GUNS&AMMO

Guide to
AK-47s

GUNS&AMMO

Guide to
AK-47s

**A COMPREHENSIVE GUIDE TO SHOOTING,
ACCESSORIZING, AND MAINTAINING
THE MOST POPULAR FIREARM IN THE WORLD**

EDITORS OF GUNS & AMMO

INTRODUCTION BY ERIC R. POOLE

Skyhorse Publishing

Skyhorse Publishing books may be purchased in bulk at special discounts for sales promotion, corporate gifts, fund-raising, or educational purposes. Special editions can also be created to specifications. For details, contact the Special Sales Department, Skyhorse Publishing, 307 West 36th Street, 11th Floor, New York, NY 10018or info@skyhorsepublishing.com.

Skyhorse® and Skyhorse Publishing® are registered trademarks of Skyhorse Publishing, Inc.®, a Delaware corporation.

Visit our website at www.skyhorsepublishing.com.

10 9 8 7 6 5 4 3 2

Library of Congress Cataloging-in-Publication Data is available on file.

Cover design by Tom Lau
Cover photo credit: Rock River Arms

Print ISBN: 978-1-5107-1309-3
Ebook ISBN: 978-1-5107-1315-4

Printed in China

TABLE OF CONTENTS

Introduction by Eric R. Poole   vii

PART I: FEATURES

Meet Mr. Kalashnikov: A Look at the Hero of the Soviet Union
  and His Rifle—David M. Fortier   2

Red Army Night Fighters, Part I: The Untold Story of Russia's Secret
  Night Vision Programs—Doug Ford   8

Red Army Night Fighters, Part II: The Untold Story of Russa's
  Secret Night Vision Programs—Doug Ford   18

The All-American AK: A Former Spetsnaz Soldier Reviews a
  Cross-Section of Off-the-Shelf Kalashnikovs—Marco Vorobiev   27

AKs Around the World: A Pictorial Look at Variants of This Classic
  Design—Tim Pack   32

PART II: STEP-BY-STEPS

Building an AK: Back to the Future, Mechanics-Wise—Patrick Sweeney   41

Cracking the AK Combination Tool: A Combo Tool Came with Your Rifle,
  but Do You Know How to Use It?—Steve Miles   48

AK Armorer: An AK Front Sight Tool Everyone Should Take
  to the Field—Gus Norcross   53

AK Armorer: Removing the AK-47 Rear Sight—Gus Norcross   54

AK Armorer: Disassembly of the AK Bolt—Gus Norcross   55

Zeroing the AK-47: A Step-by-Step Guide to Sighting-In Your AK
  by the Soviet Textbook—James Tarr   56

AK Armorer: Disassembly of the AK Fire Control Group—Gus Norcross   60

PART III: GEAR AND ACCESSORIES

AK Forearms and Rails: When You Really Have to Have Lots
  of Stuff—Patrick Sweeney   64

Ammunition for the Avtomat Kalashnikova: A Tale of Two
    Cartridges—Peter G. Kokalis 72

Feeding Your Kalashnikov: Identifying and Collecting AK-47
    Mags—Edward T. McLean 80

Improving the 7.62x39: The Performance of This 1943-Vintage
    Round Can Easily Be Improved—Zak Smith 92

Accessorize Your AK: Midwest Industries AK-47/74
    Handguard—David M. Fortier 96

US Palm AK-47 Accessories: Making the AK-47 More
    User-Friendly—Doug Larson 100

Mounting a Red Dot on Your Avtomat: Three Ways to Add a
    Modern Reflex Sight to Your AK—David M. Fortier 106

Put a Muzzle on It: Devices for Minimizing Felt Recoil and Flash
    on a 7.62 AK—Brian Edwards 112

PART IV: BUILDING AND TRAINING

California Legal: How a California Resident Can Legally Own
    an AK Variant—Timothy Yan 120

Building the Accurate Kalashnikov Shooter: Precision Is More
    Than a Quality Rifle and Scope—Gabe Suarez 127

The Kalashnikov Sniper: You Can Afford to Build a Capable Rifle
    to Address Most Engagements—Gabe Suarez 132

Snubnose Kalashnikov: Can the AK Fill the Role
    of a PDW?—Gabe Suarez 138

A View from the Other Side: Introducing Reality into
    Firearms Training—Mark Vorobiev 144

Cold Winter Training at Behind Lines: Learn to Prepare Your Rifle
    and Kit for the Chilly Extreme—Mark Vorobiev 150

Gunfighting with the Kalshnikov: Learn to Run the AK the Way It Was
    Intended—Gabe Suarez 156

Automats in Austin: Reverse Enginerring the AK Gunfight with Sonny
    Puzikas—Steve Miles 162

INTRODUCTION

Whether it was out of jealousy or disgust, I was the hoarder—the guy in the unit who some troops detested. However, I did have tough competition in my company gunny. I was thankful to be assigned to a light armored vehicle unit because I didn't have to hump seabags of war trophies along my entire journey, and even more thankful that I was assigned to be the scout for my company's executive officer—that generally meant that I'd have more space in my vehicle and I'd see action before the gunny's supply train could catch up and declare dibs on battlefield remnants.

Looking back, I don't know why finding small arms and AKs was so exciting. I knew that I'd eventually have to return them. Nonetheless, I compiled quite an impressive collection in ten months, logged each detail into a Green Monster for record, and studied them against a Peter Kokalis book I had brought with me for downtime.

Since that experience, I have been trying to recollect what some grinning POAG took from me at US Customs in Kuwait. Obviously, my current attempt will never be fully satisfied. I'll never again claim ownership of an Iraqi Tabuk or any other full-auto Com-Block AK. Regardless, my collecting is an ongoing feat to acquire the US-legal equivalents and give them treatments to make them more closely resemble my long-lost battlefield pick-ups.

My Green Monster shows that I possessed three AK underfolders: a Soviet AKMS manufactured in 1971, an Iraqi Tabuk, and a Romanian model that was dated 1987. Though I can find no regular army in the world that still issues an underfolder to its soldiers, my marines did come against a number of conscripted Iraqis who carried them, which is why I consider the underfolder still relevant to a collector of modern militaria.

The underfolders were a touch of class in the eyes of my enemy. It offered the utility desired by the poor bastard who had to smash and splinter his wood stock to achieve the same shoot-from-the-hip handling. The Cold War days of arming poorly trained and ill-equipped third-world regimes are over. Today, Romania is brushing off the negative association with communism, and doing it by supporting coalition forces in the war against terrorism.

Romania donated a thousand AKM rifles and ammunition to the new Afghan National Army after the United States-led force knocked the Taliban from power. It has also deployed troops to Iraq and the highly trained mountain infantry and with a platoon of military police to train the Afghan National Guard. These soldiers are still armed with Romanian-built AK and AKM rifles that were largely manufactured by the same Cugir factory that stamps the WASR underfolder I purchased through jgsales.com—and that's as close as I'll ever get to owning this part of history.

As you'll see in the pages of this book, we showcase the history of the AK and how it has been used in Russia and around the world. We also cover topics like step-by-step modifications, ammo, accessories, and tactics. There are chapters like Gabe Suarez's coverage of gunfighting and personal defense; Zak Smith's deep-dive into collecting AK magazines; and Marco Vorobiev's field test of various off-the-shelf AKs. We wanted to represent a cross-section of all things AK-related, and we hope you find the features in the *Guns & Ammo Guide to AK-47s* interesting and useful.

Eric R. Poole

PART I
FEATURES

MEET MR.

Mikhail Kalashnikov sits in his home discussing his design with the author. A hero in his own country, his rifle is known and respected around the globe.

KALASHNIKOV

A look at the hero of the Soviet Union and his rifle.

Text and photos by David M. Fortier

What sets Mikhail Kalashnikov apart from other famous rifle designers? That's a fairly simple question to answer. No other weapons designer in history has breathed life into a rifle that has been manufactured even remotely in the quantities of Kalashnikov's Avtomat. With estimates starting at 50 million, the Kalashnikov assault rifle simply has no peer in units manufactured.

The natural question to follow is why has this Russian design, scoffed at by many in the West, proven so popular and long lived? To understand the rifle, one must first understand its designer. For if one understands Mikhail Kalashnikov, the secret of his Avtomat is revealed.

To reach the beginning of our story we must travel back in time to the days of the Russian Revolution. On November 10, 1919, in a small rural village of Kurya in the Altai Territory, Mikhail Timofeevich

Born the son of a peasant, Mikhail Kalashnikov went on to become the most famous weapons designer of our time. His rifle is seen on the flags of six countries and in some regions of Africa "Kalash" is a common name for a boy. Photo courtesy Soviet Archives.

Kalashnikov was born. His parents, Timofei and Alexandra Frolovna Kalashnikov, were peasants and he was born into a very hard life. Of his mother's 19 children (he being the 10th) only eight survived.

The world he grew up in was located 1,864 miles east of Moscow on the border of southern Siberia and Mongolia. Winter here is very cold while summer is short, hot and often dry. Life was hard for the young Kalashnikov, he worked as a horse driver starting at the age of seven doing field work for a neighbor. His labor lasted from sunrise until 11 p.m. during the height of summer. It was at this early age that he learned the true price of bread.

Even so, he grew up the same as most children. He laughed, sang and played. At times he got in trouble, such as after falling

through thin ice while skating or when caught smoking as a young boy. He had his first teenage crush, a young girl named Zina, and took to writing poetry. While those who knew him at this time thought he would eventually become a poet, he developed another passion as a young boy. This was investigating mechanical devices. Anything mechanical he could get his hands on he took apart, and if something was broke he tried to fix it.

Eventually he ran into some trouble with the local authorities and left his family behind. He traveled to Kazakhstan with a friend and soon went to work at the Matai railroad station. Within a short time the Young Communist League had taken note of his hard work and enthusiasm. This led to a promotion to the position of technical secretary of the political department of the Turkistan-Siberian railway.

In the fall of 1938 Kalashnikov was drafted into the Workers and Peasants Red Army (RKKA). At his draft board he stated that he was technically minded and knew something of mechanical engineering. In doing so he managed to be assigned as a tank driver in the Kiev special military region. Unfortunately, his company's Sergeant-Major took a dislike to the young man, and made his life very hard. However, in the end Kalashnikov won him over, and it was here in his armored unit that he first displayed his ability as a designer.

First he invented a fixture that made firing a TT-33 service pistol more convenient from a tank's pistol port. Then he went on to design an inertia revolution counter that kept track of how many rounds had been fired from a tank's gun, along with a device that logged a tank's running time.

It was the latter device that started him on his way as a successful designer. His work caught the attention of no less a person than General of the Army Georgy Konstantinovich Zhukov. Impressed by what he saw, Zhukov ordered Kalashnikov be sent to Leningrad in June 1941 for the implementation of his invention. However Nazi Germany's invasion put an end to this. With his country suddenly under attack, Kalashnikov left Leningrad and made his way back to his unit, the 24th Tank Regiment. At this stage in the war he, like most, was confident of a quick victory over the fascist invaders. He managed to rejoin his unit at a small railroad station near Kharkov. Here he was promoted to the rank of Senior Sergeant and given command of a T-34.

Senior Sergeant Kalashnikov first went into action in September of 1941. Fighting at the far reaches of Bryansk, his armored unit became hotly engaged with the 16th Panzer Division. During this huge armored engagement the Soviets inflicted heavy losses on the Germans. Fate would not smile on his unit long. During a counter-attack in early October Kalashnikov watched as his company commander's tank took a direct hit. A second later he was blinded by a bright flash as his own tank was put out of action. Knocked unconscious, he awoke much later badly wounded. When his T-34 had been destroyed a piece of its armor had been blown through his left shoulder.

Kalashnikov again escaped death when a German unit massacred his convoy of unarmed wounded while they were being evacuated to the rear. Caught behind enemy lines, Kalashnikov and two other survivors walked 15 kilometers before they received medical attention from a civilian doctor. They rested for a few days, then trudged for seven days to reach Soviet lines.

Due to the severity of his wounds Kalashnikov spent a long convalescence in Evacuation Hospital 1133 in Yelets. It was while recovering that he became determined to design a sound submachine gun. In the hospital he heard wounded soldiers complain about having to share rifles due to chronic shortages. The men also spoke bitterly about the lack of automatic weapons in general, and of submachine guns in particular.

Milled receiver or stamped receiver, long or short barrel, 5.45x39mm or 7.62x39mm, a Kalashnikov is unmistakable in profile no matter its model or caliber. It was designed to be extremely reliable, simple to operate, and easy to manufacture.

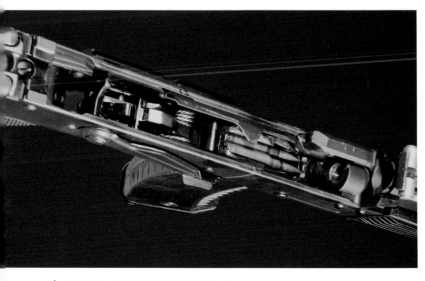

Like in so many wars before, Russian soldiers were being sent off to fight with little more than the courage in their hearts. Kalashnikov resolved to change this. After numerous discussions with other wounded soldiers he decided that he would design a lightweight and reliable submachine gun that was simple to manufacture. He not only accomplished this, but after being given a six-month sick leave, he returned to the Matai railway depot. Here, with considerable help, he produced a functioning model.

While his first design never made it past the prototype stage, it caught the attention of the leading Soviet small arms designer of the time, Anatoliy A. Blagonravov. Realizing Kalashnikov was a novice in the field of weapons design, Blagonravov suggested he receive a proper technical education and continue in this field. So Kalashnikov was given the opportunity to study the history of firearms and the intricacies of design. When the Soviets began looking to replace their obsolete submachine guns with a modern

7.62x39mm assault rifle (Avtomat), Kalashnikov began.

His concept for the new weapon was based directly upon his wartime experiences. He wanted it to be not only reliable, lightweight and compact but also simple to build and operate. Leading a design team, and receiving advice from senior colleagues, he had a prototype ready by 1946. This evolved into the famous Avtomat Kalashnikova 1947 as we know it today.

Officially adopted on June 18, 1949, the AK-47 soon proved to be an incredibly rugged and reliable automatic weapon. With a length of approximately 34.5 inches and a weight of 9.4 pounds, it is a quick-handling weapon. Selective-fire, it utilizes a rotating bolt operated by a long stroke gas piston attached to the bolt carrier. Feed is from detachable double-column 30 round box magazines. These hold a true intermediate cartridge, the 7.62x39mm M43, which is similar in concept to the German 7.92x33mm Kurz. This round gives the rifle adequate penetration and terminal performance at normal infantry engagement ranges, yet allows it to be fairly controllable on full auto.

Sights consist of a simple unprotected tangent rear adjustable in 100-meter increments out to 800 meters. The front is a protected post, front-adjustable for windage and elevation. Controls consist of a simple selector lever on the right side of the weapon's receiver, and a paddle magazine release. When the selector is placed in its uppermost position the weapon is on Safe, the action is sealed, and the bolt cannot be withdrawn far enough to chamber a round. In the center position the weapon is on Fully Automatic, and fires at cyclic rate of approximately 600 rpm. In the lowest position the weapon is on Semi-Automatic. Initially this model was fitted with wooden furniture, and was not provided with a bayonet.

When first adopted the rifle was built on a stamped sheet metal receiver. Structural problems led to a machined steel receiver being introduced in 1951. Approved in 1953 this model weighed 8.4 pounds, had a butt of smaller dimensions that attached differently and it accepted a bayonet. This is the classical AK-47 that most think of. Unfortunately its receiver, machined from a forged billet of steel, was time-consuming and expensive to manufacture.

The AK-47 was "modernized" to become the AKM (Avtomat Kalashnikova

Kalashnikov was a T-34 tank commander at the beginning of the war and saw heavy combat before being seriously wounded when his tank was put out of action in October of 1941. Photo courtesy Soviet Archives.

Modernizirovannyi-Modernized Kalashnikov Assault Rifle) in 1959. The most significant change was the return to an improved stamped-steel receiver. Other changes included the addition of a hammer trip retarder, receiver impact point changed from the right front to the left front, sighting plane extended from 800 to 1000 meters and the furniture was changed to resin-bonded-plywood. The extensive use of stamped parts reduced the weapon's empty weight to just 7.4 pounds. At this time a multi-purpose knife bayonet replaced the older model bayonet then in service.

When the U.S. introduced the 5.56x45mm cartridge in Vietnam, the Soviets were quick to grasp its attributes. Realizing the potential of a small-caliber high velocity round, they developed a

low-recoil impulse cartridge of their own, the 5.45x39mm. At this time the Soviets had done sufficient research to desire a revolutionary rather than evolutionary step in small arms. During the middle to late 1960s a series of experimental rifles designed by Youriy Alexandrov were produced that eliminated felt recoil via a balanced counter-recoil system. Offering a greater hit probability across its entire effective range than the AKM or M16 series was capable of, his AL7 was a great step forward. However, at this time the

The AK-47 was chambered for the 7.62x39mm M43 cartridg, which bridged the gap between the 7.62x25mm (L) utilized in pistols and subguns, and the full-power 7.62x54R (R).

The original AK-47 was built on a stamped-steel receiver. However, problems led to the introduction of a receiver machined from a forged billet, which was used until the AKM was introduced in 1959. Soviet fire-control parts were also machined from steel billets.

Soviet Union did not have the finances to switch to an entirely new rifle design.

Rather than replacing the AKM with a different design, a new small-caliber version was developed. Chambered for the 5.45x39mm M74 cartridge it was adopted as the AK74 (Avtomat Kalashnikova 1974) in 1974.

This small-caliber assault rifle differs from the AKM in more than just caliber. The most noticeable feature of this model is a prominent, and very effective, muzzle brake. The foresight bracket is different with a lug at its rear for the cleaning rod and a threaded cylinder at its front for the muzzle brake. Another change is the addition of an oval spring washer at the rear of the gas tube and handguard assembly. Plus, the bolt carrier has been lightened, a protrusion added, and the bolt itself is smaller with minute changes. Lastly, a grooved rubber buttplate is

The genesis of the AK-47 was Nazi Germany's invasion of Soviet Russia in 1941. Senior Sergeant Kalashnikov first went into action in September of 1941 near Bryansk. Photo courtesy of the Department of Defense.

mounted. This model tips the scales at 7.2 pounds.

The AK74 saw heavy combat in Afghanistan and proved to be a capable and accurate combat rifle. Eventually the AK74 was updated to become the AK74M (Avtomat Kalashnikova 1974 Modernizirovannyi-Modernized 1974 Kalashnikov Assault Rifle). Adopted in 1991, it features a side folding stock and furniture made from a glass-filled polyamide material. Barrel length is approximately 16.37 inches, and weight is 7.4 pounds. In addition, a rail for mounting optics is provided on the left side of the rifle's receiver. This is the current service rifle of the Federal Russian Army.

When the Russians shifted to the 5.45x39mm M74 round they quickly found that many of their traditional foreign customers were no longer placing orders. Countries that had used the older 7.62x39mm M43 AKMs in heavy combat were reluctant to switch from the older, well-proven cartridge. It is also interesting to note that Kalashnikov himself has a strong disdain for the 5.45x39mm M74 cartridge, much preferring the original 7.62x39mm M43. So the Russians, in an attempt to bolster sagging sales, introduced the AK100 series. AK, of course, still stands for Avtomat Kalashnikova, while 100 is an old coded designation of the IZHMASH Armory. Using the AK74M as a base, rifles and carbines in 5.56x45 (AK-101, 102) and 7.62x39 (AK-103, 104) were introduced along with a carbine in 5.45x39 (AK-105). So the new designation gives both the model and manufacturer.

The Kalashnikov series is very much a product of the designer's times and experiences. It is simple to manufacture,

requiring only basic machinery, and so is easily produced in huge quantities. This allows it to be used to arm large armies in the case of total war. Not only that, but it's also relatively inexpensive to produce. Due to this it will not drain a poor country's economy. Extremely rugged and reliable, it will continue to function in even the harshest of environments. Easy to operate, training even uneducated troops to use the Kalashnikov is not difficult. In the hands of well-trained troops it has proven to be highly effective. While an aging design from a previous generation, the Kalashnikov will soldier on well into the future.

Lunch with the Legend

Exiting the van we headed up the walk towards the summer home of Mikhail Timofeevich Kalashnikov. After traveling thousands of miles my friends and I had finally arrived at the home of the Grand old Man himself. In Russia he is a legend, a hero of the people known to every school child. I knew the legend; now I was about to meet the man.

The door opened and he met us on his porch. Dressed in Reed pattern camouflage pants and a light shirt, Mikhail Kalashnikov warmly welcomed us to his summer home. Our hosts introduced us and we followed him inside. The home sits in the midst of an attractive and well-kept garden with many flowers and exotic plants. The cottage was floored and walled in nicely finished pine boards. Rustic, it was obviously the home of a man who loved the outdoors.

We removed our shoes and he invited us into his living room. There we settled ourselves around him and presented him with a few gifts. Mr. Kalashnikov is a serious knife collector, so we felt a presentation grade Ka-Bar would be appropriate. In Russian tradition, he reached into his pocket and pulled out a coin which he gave in return. Along with the knife, we gave him letters from American firearms enthusiasts who owned various versions of his rifle and respected his design. As a Life member of the NRA, this made him smile—and he exhorted us to keep the anti-gunners at bay.

Then Mark Vorobiev, a veteran of the Soviet Army, emotionally thanked him for designing the rifle that had saved his life during his service in Afghanistan. This greatly moved him, and you could see the tears well up in his eyes as he nodded knowingly. You could tell that it was for a moment such as this that he had worked so hard around the clock so many years ago. "My intentions were to build a rifle to protect and defend my Motherland. A simple and utterly reliable rifle, which our young soldiers could trust and depend on. Today some people accuse me of making a weapon of war, a weapon used by terrorists. That was never my intention. I designed my rifle only to defend my country."

While Simonov's handy 7.62x39mm SKS carbine was adopted in 1945, it was soon relegated to ceremonial use by the adoption of the AK-47.

Over the next few hours we had a chance to get to know and dine with the man behind the legend. A gifted storyteller, he made us feel right at home with colorful tales from his past. He grew up in exciting times, and talked about his youth, his days as an aspiring weapons designer, and, of course, his weapons. He expounded on how he felt the Soviet switch from the 7.62x39mm cartridge to the 5.45x39mm was a huge mistake. And he reminisced about time spent with Eugene Stoner, who became a dear friend before he passed away.

As we sat discussing firearms and sharing stories, I became impressed by how down-to-earth Mr. Kalashnikov is. Originally I had not been sure what to expect, but in the end my expectations didn't matter: He far exceeded them with his friendly open attitude and fatherly demeanor. When our time together was over all too soon, I came away with the impression that Mikhail Kalashnikov is one of the few legends who actually lives up to his reputation.

Kalashnikov is also the father of one of the best GPMG in the world, the PKM. Not only is it extremely reliable, but it's also significantly lighter than our own M240B. Photo courtesy U.S. Army.

Kalashnikov rifles armed the Soviet Empire, as well as countries around the world. Here a Romanian soldier is armed with a folding-stock PM Model 65. Photo courtesy U.S. Army.

NIGHT FIGHTERS

THE UNTOLD STORY OF RUSSIA'S SECRET NIGHT VISION PROGRAMS.

PART I

In 1949, Russia fielded what is generally considered to be the most successful infantry rifle of the 20th century. This is no great secret today, but at the time of its introduction the AK47 assault rifle and its ancillary equipment were the product of highly classified military projects conducted during that tense period of world history. It was the Cold War.

These secret R&D programs were undertaken at great effort and expense. They involved some revolutionary new technologies, not the least of which was a new field in electro-optics. This branch of science eventually changed the face of modern combat and encompasses some of the most important military applications imaginable. This includes vital components used in spacecraft and missile guidance systems, navigation, rangefinding, target detection and recognition, missile defense, radiation sensing, nuclear testing and weapons aiming systems.

However, the scope of this article will focus specifically on Soviet applications of optoelectronics developed as night vision devices for combat use on Kalashnikov-designed small arms.

1944–45: SOVIET-GERMAN NVD TECHNOLOGIES

Even as the Soviet war machine rolled into the burning ruins of Germany's capital during the closing actions of World War II, a massive effort was already underway to "liberate" important German scientists and salvage surviving examples of Hitler's wonder weapons for further research in Moscow. Conversely, the Allies were also racing to take advantage of German breakthroughs. One relatively unknown new technology used by Germany was the application of infrared (IR) devices as night-time aiming aids for small arms.

VAMPIR

In 1944, the Germans successfully fielded the first example of such a device to see actual

Former Soviet special operations weapons: The Kalashnikov AKML infantry rifle and the RPKL light machine gun.

BY DOUG FORD

combat. Code-named Vampir, the Zielgerät 1229 (ZG 1229) infrared night vision rifle sight was mated to another revolutionary Nazi design, the StG.44 assault rifle. This man-portable night-fighting system would see action for the first time in February 1945, and some of that combat opposed the Red army.

The end result was, of course, a case of too little too late, but the concept was sound and the Allies soon realized technological advances of this type could tip the balance of power in a future conflict.

It would be quite unfair, however, to assume that the story of Soviet electro-optical development started with the mere cloning of captured German systems. Russian engineers had begun pioneering this field, on their own, as early as 1935. This was partially forced upon them since international cooperation in this field of science had all but ceased to exist due to emerging military applications and the resulting secrecy it created. In any case, by 1940 the Soviets were producing their first optoelectronic image converters (EOC) and introducing a great number of practical military uses for IR-based technology into their military. These involved signaling and navigation, air- and seaborne homing and direction-finding beacons, infrared target identification and illumination, as well as aircraft landing aids.

ISKRA

In 1944, the USSR was able to test its first domestic portable infrared weapons sight, code-named Iskra and type classified as the SPN-1. This NV system was intended for use on the M91/30 bolt-action sniper rifle, although it likely saw experimentation with other small arms. It was eventually issued to engineering corps personnel during the later part of World War II.

Iskra operated in a similar manner to the Vampir system, although it was less integrated and used a more cumbersome two-man operating format. According to Soviet sources, it did not, however, see combat during the war.

After the war, little time was wasted in various laboratories and workshops within the Soviet industrial complex in an effort to recover possible value from German research programs. Soviet specialists who were sent to Germany to evaluate firsthand the status of Hitler's night vision programs were impressed by the high

quality of the image converters and the organization involved in their assembly. The findings were quickly incorporated into existing Soviet NVD projects.

1946–49: AVTOMAT KALASHNIKOV AND RESEARCH INSTITUTE 801

Thus we come to the interesting story of Kalashnikov Night Fighters, which begins in 1946. In that year, M.T. Kalashnikov was given approval by Moscow to proceed with development of the first production-model Avtomat Kalashnikov, Russia's first true production assault rifle. The AK offered both a high degree of firepower and compact size, virtues that fit in perfectly with the Red army's traditional tactic of massed firepower. These characteristics also made it the perfect choice for clandestine night operations conducted by irregular military forces.

In the same year, the Council of People's Commissars also formed Research Institute 801, or NII-801. Based in Moscow, this secret design bureau was made up of top electro-optical and IR techniques engineers and scientists and included laboratories in the various applied sciences. It also eventually included facilities for the small-scale pilot production of electro-optical systems.

A 1958-dated Soviet training poster for the NSP-3 illustrates the rivet attachment of the AKN optical mounting dovetail and the proper alignment for engagement with the sight's clamp assembly.

A restored 1958-dated AKN with NSP-2 infrared night vision sight fitted for deployment. Note the limited-production early-pattern folding wire bipod.

Looking down the barrel of the AKMBL, you can see the Cyrillic-marked metal plate that denotes range settings for use on 7.62x39mm AKML and RPKL rifles.

This institute, under various names and assigned to various military departments, would be directly involved in almost every important aspect of Soviet night vision technology development. Its primary mission was the development, design and testing of all types of electro-optical devices, which would then be manufactured by the various established optical production plants of the USSR.

By 1949, the AK47 was placed into series production, and plans were quickly underway to adapt the new rifle for use as a limited-production night-fighting rifle. To that end, Research Institute 801 busied itself in the early 1950s creating a whole new line of night vision scopes for use with the AK as well as many other small arms.

1954: THE FIRST KALASHNIKOV NIGHT FIGHTERS

All of these early NVD optics are classified in modern times as being Generation 0 "Active" IR sights. The Soviet units developed in the 1950s used a silver-oxygen-cesium photoelectric cathode image converter tube, which was sensitive to infrared (IR) radiation, a form of light that is invisible to the naked eye. The sight was tuned to convert IR into visible light, which would then be presented to the end user in a usable form. The focus of the light was generally handled by electrostatic means. These early electro-optical converters provided very little gain.

A relatively conventional lens system provided magnification of the FOV, while an illuminated reticle presented a central aiming marker. On Soviet models, the aiming marker was traditionally an inverted chevron flanked by horizontal bars. These bars were used for gauging windage and estimating range, especially on vehicular targets.

These early "Gen 0" devices usually relied on powerful IR spotlights to illuminate the battlefield and detect targets. This provided excellent performance in the immediate area, but had several very distinct drawbacks. For instance, the maximum effective operating range of the sight was limited by the range of the IR flood lamps. Also, having to provide operating power for a rather inefficient early image converter, the reticle illuminator and the high-drain IR floodlight meant the battery was subsequently quite bulky, heavy and short-lived.

However, the main disadvantage could get you killed, because once enemy forces were equipped with even the simplest IR detection devices, the unlucky operator of a night vision scope projecting a bright beam of IR light across a modern

Receiver comparisons of (right to left) the AKN, RPKL and AKML. The AKN uses a one-piece rail design, while the others are two-piece assemblies.

battlefield made him a primary target for snipers. It must be remembered that in 1954 these were necessary evils since this type of system was state of the art, even in the U.S.

NAP-1

Russia's first issue Kalashnikov night vision scope was the NAP-1 (ночной автоматный прицел, or Avtomat Night Sight-1st model), which was developed around 1954, entering limited military production before 1956. NAP-1 was actually designed not only for the new Kalashnikov, but also for the 7.62mm RPD light machine gun and the RPG-2 rocket-propelled grenade launcher.

NAP-1 featured a 2.2X telescopic riflescope lens assembly providing a nine-degree field of view (FOV). This lens system and IR-range electro-optical image converter were housed in a cast alloy tubular body. Unlike the World War II-era Iskra sniper scope, the IR projector lamp assembly on NAP-1 was permanently attached to the top of the sight itself. A large electronics compartment containing the power converters was integral to the scope.

The new optic also employed an adjustable dovetail clamp assembly designed for easy mounting onto the left-hand side on any one of several parent rifles, which included a special version of the AK47, the AKN. The "N" suffix (ночным прицелом, or Night Sight), of course, denoted its night-fighting capabilities.

A one-piece, milled-steel, dovetailed optics rail was permanently attached to the left-hand side of the AKN receiver by way of five flush-mounted rivets that were designed to accept the clamp on the scope. Other than the fact that the rear sling swivel was relocated to the bottom of the buttstock to make room for this, there were no other apparent alterations.

Due to the large size and weight of the battery assembly, it was carried separately in a backpack arrangement in the same way as the German Vampir system. The power supply was connected to the scope during operations by a flexible multi-conductor power cable, which could be quickly disconnected.

Even before the full potential of the NAP-1 could be determined, input from various field

The Vyatskie Polyani-produced RPKL/RPKN scope rail assembly is similar to that of the Izhevsk-made AKML, but has consideration for use with side-folding-stocked RPKSL rifles.

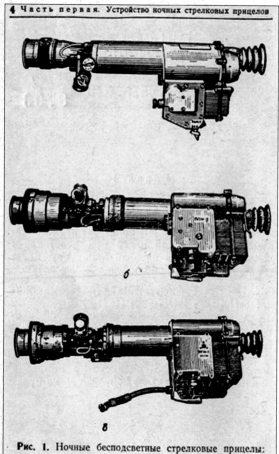

4 Часть первая. Устройство ночных стрелковых прицелов

Рис. 1. Ночные бесподсветные стрелковые прицелы:
а — НСП-3; б — ППН-3; в — ПГН-1

tests suggested several needed improvements. Research Institute 801 had already been developing more advanced packages, much of the research at this time concentrated on miniaturization and battery efficiency.

NSP-2

In 1956, the institute released a newly upgraded version of its Kalashnikov night vision scope under the designation NSP-2 (ночной стрелковый прицел, or Night Gun Sight, 2nd model). This model was quickly adopted by the Soviet military.

NSP-2 was a direct replacement for NAP-1, and initial issue to specialized troops occurred by late 1957. The new sight was still a Generation-0 IR-based device and used the same basic format as the earlier NAP-1. It also looked similar and had a comparable telescopic magnification of 2.1X with an eight-degree FOV.

Otherwise, it was an improvement in almost every possible area of its engineering, i.e. more effective, reliable, usable, portable and ergonomic. It would be kept in domestic production, without major changes, for almost 10 years and for almost a decade longer as a license-produced model elsewhere.

A long list of upgrades were included in its design, most notably a welcomed reduction in overall combat weight through replacement of the backpack-carried battery (5.1Kg) of NAP-1 for a smaller, lighter, belt-carried 6.2-volt unit (2.0Kg). The new power source provided roughly four hours of continuous operation.

The objective tube was fitted with a new sheet-metal lens cap, manually adjustable to limit incoming light. It was removed during normal night operations. Direct light was always a threat that could permanently damage the image converters of NVD, and early units were designed without any type of protection against such events. Closing off the objective entrance allowed for testing the operation of the electronics package during daylight hours.

The IR projector lamp assembly was now fitted with a hinged metal cover that would protect it from damage, and the battery cable arrangement was rearranged for ergonomic reasons. Also, the electronics layout of the power converters and battery box were modified to ease replacement of the electronic components.

This Soviet small-arms NV model lineup was taken from a 1970-dated Soviet military manual. This manual was marked "Secret." Top to bottom: the NSP-3, PPN-3 and PGN-1.

Both the NAP-1 and NSP-2 were designed without a specific cartridge calibration. Therefore, a ballistic chart was embossed on the inspection cover to provide instructions on how to properly dial in the range for use on AK and RPD rifles.

With the NSP-2 installed, the AKN weighed about 7.45Kg and was rated to provide satisfactory target acquisition out to a maximum of 150 to 250 meters. This, however, depended a great deal on environmental conditions and target size.

PPN-2

The overall size and weight of the NSP-2 system was minimized to make it manageable on infantry rifles and meet the requirements of a typical foot soldier's maximum combat load, but Research Institute 801 determined that a heavier, longer-range model could be employed for use with larger rifles in the Soviet arsenal, many of which were mounted on wheeled carriages and motorized vehicles or deployed in static point defense positions using tripods and bipods. For these roles, an upgraded version of NSP-2 was developed, providing extended range using more powerful IR projectors and more robust battery packs.

The result was the PPN-2 (пулемётный прицел ночной, or Machinegun Night Sight, 2nd model), a 3.5X telescopic Generation-0 NVD intended as a replacement for the SPN-1-based, 1946-era PPN-1. Unlike the smaller NSP-2, the PPN-2 carried its heavy-duty, 12.3-volt wet-cell battery directly attached to the scope. Overall weight increased to a hefty 101/2Kg. However, all of the upsizing provided an improved maximum effective target acquisition range of about 300 to 350 meters.

PPN-2 was originally developed for use on the Degtyaryov RP-46 light machine gun, the Goryunov SG-43 medium machine gun, the SGM heavy machine gun and the B-12 recoil-less rifle. It was also pressed into service on the PK machine gun in the early 1960s.

1959–65: THE RESEARCH INSTITUTE OF APPLIED PHYSICS

Between 1959 and 1963, Soviet Russia introduced a new wave of completely updated infantry rifles, many of which were all-new designs that eventually proved to be some of the most successful examples of their various classifications. Notable were the AKM modernized Kalashnikov assault rifle, the PK general-purpose machine gun, the RPK light machine gun, the SVD sniper rifle and the RPG-7 rocket-propelled grenade launcher. All of these would eventually receive night vision treatments.

During these times, the Russians also began a technology transfer program in tandem with licensed production of various Soviet weapons systems, including electro-optical production, based in satellite countries. Beginning in the 1960s, domestic versions of Soviet night vision devices were manufactured in Poland, Czechoslovakia, East Germany and Hungary.

In 1965, a reorganization of the defense ministries of the USSR resulted in Research Institute 801 being placed under the Ministry of Defense Industry. At that time, the institute was renamed the Research Institute of Applied Physics. This was the beginning of a major expansion in the responsibilities of the electro-optical division, and by this time more than 100 separate facilities were involved in the development and manufacture of night vision devices under the guidance of NIIPF.

In the early 1960s, the first series of new, modernized Kalashnikov night-fighting rifles based on the AKM and RPK simply used the existing NSP-2 sights, which were carried over from the AKN and RPDN. However, since they were assembled using sheetmetal receivers, the new AKMN and RPKN were outfitted with a heavier-duty two-piece steel scope base consisting of a lower anchor plate riveted to the rifle and an upper dovetail rail aligned and screwed into the anchor plate. These mounted onto the left side of the receiver and, once installed, ensured a secure, stable and extremely strong platform for supporting the heavy electro-optics of the period.

GENERATION 1 NVD

Major technological advancements were not long in coming. Everything basically changed in the early 1960s when Russian engineers developed new and revolutionary solutions in the quest for better forms of electro-optical converters. The first innovation was in the form of extremely efficient multi-alkali photoelectric cathode intensifier tubes, which produced far more gain (light amplification) and a great deal more frequency range than any other previous method. In fact, the sensitivity of these units included the visible light spectrum, which paved the way for the first passive Generation-1 NVD devices.

Soviet engineers soon discovered that coupling multiple alkali-based image intensifier tubes in series, one behind the other in a cascade formation, would result in an effective design with performance parameters suitable for military applications. These Starlight scopes amplified natural ambient lighting and thus eliminated the need for special, conspicuous active IR illuminators. In this form, the first Gen-1 night vision devices were developed and introduced into the armed forces of the USSR.

NSP-3

By 1965, development of the NSP-3 (ночной стрелковый прицел, or Night Gun Sight, 3rd model) Generation-1 passive night vision scope was completed, and the optic began entering limited service within Soviet special-purpose operating groups. The NSP-3 was equipped with a newly developed cascade-type image intensifier tube and provided 2.7X telescopic magnification. It also took advantage of magnetic focus technologies.

Modified night-fighting versions of the 7.62x39mm AKM as well as the RPK (designated as AKML and RPKL) were designed specifically for use with the NSP-3. A new long-style, slotted flash hider was provided on both models for flash protection and was necessary because adequate light "gating" protection circuitry did not exist on these early Generation-1 models. The hider was designed to keep muzzle flash from permanently burning into the image presented to the user or seriously damaging the converter tube.

Most early AKM and RPK rifles originally equipped with older, obsolete IR sights were retrofitted with the NSP-3. Folding-stock versions of both models (designated AKMSL and RPKSL) were also created, which required extensive modifications to the design of the buttstock configurations in order to clear the rail system when the stock was folded. From late 1966 onward, all newly built rifles mated with the NSP-3 were fitted with a slightly altered two-piece optics mounting rail that gave better eye-relief spacing for the new scope.

An even more specialized version of AKML rifle was outfitted for use with the PBS-1 Silent Fire Device. These weapons, designated as AKMBL and AKMSBL (folding stock), were equipped with a fairly complex windage-adjustable dual-calibration (sonic and subsonic ammunition capable) rear sight leaf assembly and were meant for use on clandestine nighttime operations. One of their primary end users was Spetsnaz KGB.

Operating voltage for the NSP-3 was supplied by a miniaturized three-cell battery pack, housed inside a battery compartment mounted alongside the electronics compartment on the sight itself. A reticle-brightness adjustment knob and bottom-mounted on/off power toggle switch were the only electronic controls provided.

The sight was equipped with several types of mechanical light-control features. First, a removable metal diaphragm for manually adjusting the amount of light entering the device was attached

Evolution of Soviet Generation-1 cascade-tube night vision sights, top to bottom: 1967 NSP-3, 1974 NSP-3A (1PN27), 1976-era NSPU (1PN34) and 1985-era NSPUM (1PN58).

Late production changes incorporated into the NSP-3 included a simplified windage adjustment turret design, a new lever-actuated filter control and eventually, a modernized diaphragm design.

to the front portion of the objective lens housing. When fully closed, it also enabled safe daylight operations in order to zero the rifle or perform maintenance. During night operations it was normally removed.

A new five-position filter mechanism was also added, designed to improve FOV clarity and contrast under varying atmospheric conditions. This mechanism was mounted on the side of the main tube, just behind the reticle adjustment assembly. One of five filter settings could manually be chosen simply by turning a rotary selector knob. Settings were marked by Cyrillic characters and included Closed, White, Red, Yellow and Neutral, each being tailored to specific lighting and weather conditions as outlined in the military user manual.

Reticle illumination was generated by a standard-issue, replaceable PSO-1 lamp module,

which was located on the casting that also housed the large, easy-to-manipulate, target-style elevation and windage turret mechanism. The reticle was improved from the NSP-2 by the addition of two vertical hash marks, positioned to each side of the main aiming marker. These provided for better range estimation as well as being windage indicators.

Range adjustments on the NSP-3 were otherwise similar to the NSP-2, i.e. they were equal-distance increments and not calibrated to a specific ballistic curve. For this reason, as on the NSP-2, a ballistic chart was engraved on a metal plate and permanently riveted to the top of the sight, detailing use on AKML and RPKL rifles.

The NSP-3 proved to be a major improvement over the old IR sights. It's rated effective operating range was extended to about 250 to 300 meters, while its

survivability due to stealth. As it was a passive device, the shooter's position could no longer be betrayed simply through the unwise or untimely use of his own IR spotlight beams.

The NSP-3 would be the primary night vision device used on 7.62x39mm Kalashnikov rifles until the mid-1970s, and a much improved version (NSP-3A) saw service in the Soviet-Afghan War well into the 1980s. Copies were also made by Poland and Hungary.

PPN-3

As with the NSP-2, uprated versions of the NSP-3 were created for use on several types of heavy weapons in the Soviet arsenal.

The PPN-3 (пулемётный прицел ночной, or Machinegun Night Sight, 2nd model) was a 4X telescopic Generation-1 NVD designed for use on the 7.62x54R PK, PKT and later on PKM general-purpose machine guns. Mass of the sight increased to 3.65Kg, but the overall effective range also increased to about 400 meters.

As with the earlier RPDN, these machine guns were equipped with a special hinged optics rail assembly, which allowed the night sight to remain mounted but tilted away from the top cover of the firearm during reloading, clearing or servicing procedures.

The PPN-3 was also fitted with an auxiliary push-type momentary power cut-off switch that worked in tandem with a special trigger-activated lever mounted on PKN and early PKMN rifles. When the rifle was fired, the lever contacted this switch and temporarily interrupted operating power to the scope. This prevented malfunction or serious damage to the EOC during automatic fire.

PGN-1

For the first time, a special model of Soviet NV
was also created for the RPG-7 rocket-propelled grenade launcher. The PGN-1 was similar to its sister, the PPN-3, but featured a cable-actuated remote power interrupter switch to prevent damage to the converter tube from rocket motor flash.

All three models (NSP-3, PPN-3 and PGN-1) were quickly adopted and placed into service, mostly issued to special-purpose forces (Spetsnaz) of the GRU, KGB, MVD and VDV (air assault troops). These supplemented and soon replaced earlier,

Russia fielded its first AK-specific passive Starlight Scope by 1965. Weight of the resulting NSP-3 with AKML automatic rifle was about 13¾ pounds.

smaller wet-cell 4½-volt battery pack provided an improved operating life of about six hours under normal conditions. The NSP-3 had a weight of around 2.7Kg even though the power source was self-contained. This also eliminated the need for annoying external power cables or belt-carried power packs.

Even so, the main tactical advantage afforded the user was greatly improved combat

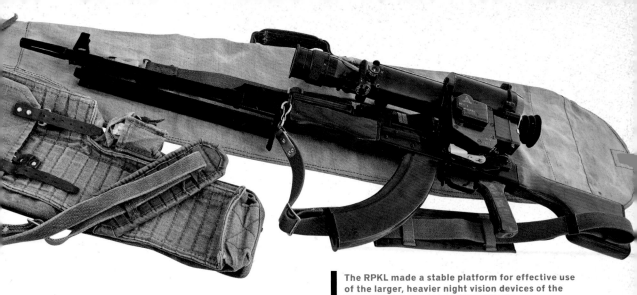

The RPKL made a stable platform for effective use of the larger, heavier night vision devices of the time. This one mounts a 1973 NSP-3A.

less satisfactory NV devices in all but secondary roles in the Soviet armed forces.

1968: SPECIAL NIGHT TROOP EXERCISES

In 1968, even while upgraded Generation-1 night sights were reaching forward operating forces, the USSR conducted a series of Special Night Troop Exercises for the purpose of evaluating the performance of "models of all series and experimental NVD." These exercises included not only man-portable small arms sights, but also much larger systems such as those mounted on vehicles.

The evaluation "revealed a number of fundamental deficiencies in the instruments, characteristic of the level of their development reached." Under ideal conditions the newer units apparently performed as well as could be expected, but the final report included a long list of rather challenging improvements requested by the military to the Research Institute and its collective laboratories.

The problem areas cited in the final reports included the overall large size and weight of the units and the small field of view. The sights were also found to perform poorly in total darkness.

Possibly the most serious complaint reported by troops in the field was the gating issue, in which the sights were incapable of satisfactorily managing errant bright lights, such as those that would be found on an active battlefield: shell blasts, tracers, muzzle flashes, headlight beams and so on.

All of this vital feedback was seriously considered by the engineers at the Institute, who went back to work finding new solutions. By 1971, serious upgrades were introduced, and by 1976 an entirely new line of effective, modernized Kalashnikov Night Fighters were readied for service, just in time for the "Big Show."

NOTE: This article is dedicated to the memory of Joe Caliri, an avid Kalashnikov arms collector, night vision enthusiast, KCA member and long-time personal friend. We lost him on 3 December, 2010. May he rest in peace.

PART II: PROJECT ORION

In the early 1970s, the Soviet Union was arguably fielding the most advanced infantry-borne military night vision devices in the world. This was the result of a massive research-and-development program undertaken by the Soviet industrial complex during the preceding two decades, which, under the technical direction of the Research Institute of Applied Physics (Institute 801), spent immense time and resources developing practical, yet highly advanced combat-capable electro-optical technologies and equipment.

In the case of Kalashnikov night-fighters, in the mid-'60s, introduction of passive first-generation devices led the way for a whole new family of truly effective and usable battlefield rifle sights. These were designed around a new type of Electro-Optical Converter (EOC), or image-intensifier tube, that amplified ambient or "starlight" radiation rather than relying on the use of artificial (IR) light sources. This technological leap enabled the development of the first truly practical infantry-borne night vision devices that allowed modern military forces to conduct effective clandestine operations under the cover of near-total darkness.

The "Special Night Troop Exercises" of 1968, however, pointed out that further improvements needed to be made. Specifically, limitations such as overall large size, heavy weight, small field of view, poor performance in total dark-ness and the unsatisfactory management of errant bright lights (such as those found on active battlefields) were cited. The Research Institute and its ancillary facilities went back to work in secret laboratories across the Soviet Union to find viable solutions.

When the Soviets rearmed with the 5.45x39mm-caliber family of rifles, including this AKS-74N, a new NSPU standardized night vision scope was developed for them.

BY DOUG FORD

NSP-3A

In 1971, an upgraded variant of the primary Kalashnikov rifle sight, named the NSP-3A (ночной стрелковый прицел, or Night Gun Sight-3rd Model-A), was introduced. The NSP-3A was also known as the 1PN27, which was its military index code as part of the newly adopted GRAU military inventory system.

The sight continued the use of the Generation 1 cascade-type image-intensifier tube with the same 2.7X magnification and used the same 4 1/2-volt wet-cell battery pack, providing an estimated operating life of about six hours. It also weighed about the same (2.7 kilograms) and provided a similarly effective target-acquisition range of about 250 to 300 meters, depending on target size and atmospheric conditions.

A new overlapping inspection cover gave it better weatherproofing, and its overall survivability was increased due to new light "gating" protection, which shielded the EOC against errant light sources, and the introduction of a new, heavily reinforced cast-alloy objective housing.

The NSP-3A was especially user-friendly because it was the first Soviet NV device dedicated specifically to 7.62x39mm rifles. To this end, the elevation-adjustment turret assembly was bullet-drop compensated for this caliber. Clandestine operators armed with an AK rifle could now dial in the estimated shooting range of a target using a handy turret thumbwheel indexed in graduations of hundreds of meters.

Changes in the outward appearance of the NSP-3A

included the addition of objective housing strengthening gussets, as well as a simplified range and elevation mechanism that did away with the thumbwheel windage adjuster. The filter lens assembly was also simplified, i.e., the options available were reduced from five (of dubious value) to just three settings that were much more manageable. The five-position rotary filter selector mechanism of the earlier style was discarded in favor of a faster and easier-to-manipulate lever-action design.

It appears that the NSP-3A was considered a success. Manufacture was conducted at the Novosibirsk Instrument Making Plant in Siberia for about seven years, until 1977, when AKM production was shuttered. Licensed production continued in other countries, notably Poland and Hungary. Polish domestic examples were issued with special night-fighting versions of the AKM, AKMS and, later, the Wz.88 Tantal rifle, from about 1977 until 1991.

During the early years of the Soviet War in Afghanistan, the NSP-3A saw a great deal of combat action, mostly among VDV (airborne) and special forces units. Among the VDV, a common load-out included three night vision riflescopes issued per platoon of about 60

A primary Spetsnaz application seen in Afghanistan included the AKMSBL, which was fitted with the PBS-1 "Silent Fire Device" and 7.62mm-specific NSP-3A. (Dummy silencer supplied by Marshall Arms.)

men. NVDs were regularly used by Soviet special forces and VDV units who were often saddled with tackling the most difficult covert operations. The primary wartime Spetsnaz application for this sight was the folding-stock AKMSL and AKMSBL, which was mated to the silent-fire-device, the PBS-1.

An AKML with an NSP-3A (1PN27) night vision scope. It features the new lever-action three-position filter selector, late-style objective-lens diaphragm and embossed NPZ logo.

CENTRAL DESIGN BUREAU TOCHPRIBOR

Design Bureau Tochpribor was established in 1972 as the primary design arm of the famous Novosibirsk Instrument Making Plant (NPZ), located in Siberia. Since the mid-'60s, the NPZ had become the primary manufacturer of small-arms night vision equipment, which included the NSP-3.

Under the umbrella of the Research Institute of Applied Physics, one of Tochpribor's first duties was to implement the finalized design and pilot-production of a newly developed universal small-arms electro-optical night vision weapon sight that would eventually replace the NSP-3, NSP-3A, PPN-3 and PGN-2 sights then in use by Soviet military forces.

NSPU

The modernized sight, the NSPU (Ночной стрелковый прицел унифицированный, or Night Gun Sight Standardized), was adopted by the military under GRAU Index 1PN34 and introduced into service in 1976.

The timing of its development and introduction was not random. In fact, the NSPU was meant as a companion device for use with a revolutionary breed of Kalashnikov assault weapons chambering the new 5.45x39mm M74 small-caliber, high-velocity round. This family of infantry rifles would eventually replace most of the older 7.62x39mm rifles and included the AK74, the RPK-74 and (by 1979) the AKS-74U assault rifle.

The NSPU had a higher magnification power (3.5X) and was developed around an upgraded, smaller-diameter Generation 1 cascade-type image-intensifier tube that offered higher levels of performance. A more advanced, efficient and lighter-weight intensifier tube design with better focusing technologies also meant it delivered a better quality field of view (FOV) with minimal fish-eye border distortion, a phenomenon that affected most, if not all, cascade-type intensifier tubes. A new 2 1/2-volt high-drain, wet-cell battery provided approximately 12 hours of continuous operation.

A large, wedge-shaped fairing was integrated into the side of the main tube body, streamlining the high-voltage block housing, which made maneuverability with the sight on the rifle less cumbersome than previous models. This also gave the

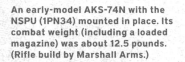

An early-model AKS-74N with the NSPU (1PN34) mounted in place. Its combat weight (including a loaded magazine) was about 12.5 pounds. (Rifle build by Marshall Arms.)

sight's main body a distinctive oval shape.

The diameter of the objective lens was increased from 52mm to 70mm, which greatly improved light-gathering and, thus, overall light-amplification performance. A large, removable objective lens diaphragm opened and closed manually by rotating its forward bezel and could be attached to the front of the objective lens housing for operating the sight in low-light or daylight conditions without doing harm to the intensifier tube.

The old, manually selectable filter system, which had been used on both the NSP-3 and 3A, was completely deleted. The only user-adjustable electronic control provided was a rotary reticle brightness adjustment knob centered on the lower portion of the front inspection cover, which also doubled as the power switch.

Improved technology also helped reduce the NSPU's total weight to 2.2 kilograms. This proved to be a very desirable quality, much liked by those tasked with lugging it around through the mountains of Afghanistan. An increased effective range (up to 400 meters) was also much better suited for use with the new high-speed, flat-shooting projectile. The NSPU also delivered a better signal-to-noise ratio, as well as increased protection from the most typical

The 1PN34 inspection cover displays an old NPZ logo (hammer and sickle with star and pentagrams), factory model nomenclature (NSPU) and sequential production serial number.

light interferences found on a modern battlefield.

As its name implies, the new "standardized" night vision sight was designed to replace a great many other rather expensive and outdated models previously issued for use on several different weapons. Having to manufacture, distribute and maintain only one model of sight adaptable to a multitude of small arms meant a reduction in costs and logistical complexity and simplified training and depot-level repairs.

The feature that enabled this flexibility was the replaceable ballistic cam, which was first introduced on this model. Now each sight could be issued with a set of cams, making fast, on-the-fly replacement in a combat zone possible.

Weapons issued with the NSPU were designated with an

"N" (ночной, or with a night sight) suffix rather than the rather mysterious "L" used with NSP-3-equipped weapons. Cam-specific NSPU applications included the AK-74N/AKS-74N, the RPK-74N/RPKS-74N, the AKMN/AKMSN, the RPKN/RPKSN, the PKMN/PKTN/PKSN, the RPG-7N and the SVDN sniper rifle. In fact, contrary to popular belief, this was actually the first time a night vision device was adopted for official use on the SVD Dragunov sniper rifle.

Thus it can be concluded that reduction in weight and the adaptability for use on multiple types of weapons were the two primary advantages of the NSPU. In Afghanistan, Russian airborne combat veterans reported that the older, heavyweight NSP-3 was eagerly replaced in the field with the much lighter NSPU—that is,

Objective lens assemblies of the NSP-3A (left) with a 52mm objective lens, an NSPU (center) with a 70mm lens and an NSPUM (right) with a 70mm lens. The removable objective lens diaphragms were used during low-light or daylight operation.

when the rare opportunity presented itself. As the war dragged on, the newer, more desirable models were available in larger numbers.

The NSPU was produced by Russia from 1976 until about 1989, most of these being assembled in Novosibirsk. Examples can be found with either the NPZ "hammer and sickle with stars and pentagram" military production symbol or Design Bureau Tochpribor's "inverted triangle-in-triangle" logo. During the Cold War, limited numbers were shipped to other Warsaw Pact members, such as East Germany, while licensed production was also carried out for a short time inside Bulgaria during the late 1980s.

SCIENTIFIC AND PRODUCTION ASSOCIATION "ORION"

In 1977, one year after the NSPU was introduced, the Soviet

A top view of an NSPUM, NSPU and NSP-3A (left to right) illustrating cosmetic differences in the intensifier tube case diameter, as well as the shape of the high-voltage block fairing.

Union reorganized the former Research Institute of Applied Physics into the Scientific and Production Association known as Orion. This new conglomerate would encompass all Soviet electro-optical research, design and manufacturing entities under one large umbrella organization. For the first time, one central organization would direct and control both the research establishments as well as the manufacturing facilities. Project Orion was meant to help Russia accelerate research and design implementation into the manufacturing centers in a more effective and timely manner.

One of the first programs Orion participated in was field evaluations of a new short-barreled Kalashnikov assault rifle, later adopted as the AKS-74U. Starting in late 1976, versions of these small assault rifles were extensively field tested in Kirovabad, Azerbaijan, by elite force units, and several of these early special-purpose Kalashnikov rifles were equipped with side-mounted optic dovetails for the attachment of NSPU sights.

This rifle model was refined and eventually adopted in 1979. Versions issued with matching

night vision (AKS-74UN) as well as night vision and PBS silencers (AKS-74UNB) were built by Izhmash (early on in very limited production) and later at Tula Arsenal, which became the primary producer after 1981.

SOVIET "SANDBOX"

During the Afghan War, the Soviet military gained firsthand practical knowledge of the important value of advanced electro-optical devices, including small-arms night sights. Some of its greatest successes on the battlefield were won through the timely use of highly trained, well-equipped airmobile specialized forces that could take full advantage of cover by night.

Military leaders soon realized that only by the effective utilization of night vision devices could their forces secure the effectiveness and superiority demanded and required for successful combat operations during the night. Practical feedback from units in the field was included in the ongoing process by Orion both to find usable technical improvements and to increase production numbers.

Innovations in the development of IR and NV technologies were taking top priority within the defense ministries as well as the military-industrial complex they controlled at this time. (One in every five Russian adults was employed in a military production plant or related research facility of one kind or another.) Through these efforts, it was not long before advanced modifications were made to existing designs.

NSPUM

By 1980, technical improvements were already becoming available for integration

Battery styles continued to advance: an NSP-3A 4.5v wet-cell pack (left), NSPU 2.5v wet-cell pack (center) and NSPUM 6.25v dry-cell assembly (right).

into new types of universal night sights, and by 1985 the Russian military introduced a refined version of the NSPU, fittingly named the NSPUM (Ночной стрелковый прицел унифицированный модернизированный, or Night Gun Sight Standardized-Modernized).

This device was officially placed into active service under GRAU Index Code 1PN58. Once again it relied on the venerable three-stage, cascade-type intensifier tube, similar to the NSPU, but it delivered what is often called Generation 1+ performance levels in terms of visibility, image quality and amplification of existing natural light.

The main body of the intensifier tube housing was slimmed down to a round cross-section by eliminating the large high-voltage block housing of previous models. This (in combination with a different-style battery compartment) made the NSPUM easily identifiable from the NSPU. Overall, NSPUM was much less bulky and quite a bit (two kilograms) lighter.

The NSPUM was a 3.5X telescopic power optic that provided a rated effective maximum range of about 400 meters for targets of various sizes. One of its best and most identifiable upgrades (due to a round rather than square-shaped battery compartment) was the switch from a rectangular wet cell to a

new 6¼-volt cylindrical multi-tablet dry-cell battery. This made maintenance much easier.

The rotary reticle brightness-adjustment/power-switch knob found on the NSPU was relocated to a more centralized position on the front inspection cover, while the larger (70mm) objective lens and removable lens diaphragm of the NSPU were carried over without change.

A set of replaceable ballistic cams was also provided with NSPUM. The actual applications intended for the sight grew in number as time went on and newer types of small arms were introduced.

Applications for this particular sight were specifically designated AK74N-2, AKS74-N-2,

A 1PN58 mounted on an AKS-74N-2 infantry rifle. The 1PN58/NSPUM was first fielded in 1985, at the height of the Afghan War.

Three primary Afghan War-era Kalashnikov NV complexes: the 7.62mm 1PN27/AKMSL (front), 5.45mm 1PN34/AKS-74N (center) and 5.45mm 1PN58/AKS-74-2 (back).

RPK74N-2, RPKN-2, AKMN-2, SVDN-2, PKN-2 and RPG-7VN-2. The number "2" suffix added to each acronym denoted that this was the second complex, or coupling, of sight and rifle that employed the same basic nomenclature and weapon type.

NSPU-3

Back in 1979, efforts on the part of Russian engineers and scientists under the authority of Orion succeeded in the development of the first Russian Generation 2 electro-optical converters, which were quickly utilized for military applications. Generation 2 electro-optical intensifier tubes relied on a new technique using Micro-Channel Technology (MCT) to greatly enhance the resolution and light amplification of

objects in the field of view of a night vision device.

Code-named Kazuar, the first Generation 2 NV scope available for Kalashnikov applications was the NSPU-3 (Ночной стрелковый прицел унифицированный, or Night Gun Sight Standardized—3rd Model), which is better known today by its military GRAU Index Code, 1PN51. This device had a magnification of 3.46X and weighed 2.1 kilograms.

The 1PN51 certainly looked different than the previous Russian NV sights, having a tall, short-barrel-shaped body in contrast to the long bazooka-like NSP-3 and NSPU. The weapon clamping system and user controls were pretty much the same, and re-placeable ballistic cams were still an important part of the standard-

issue kit. The 6¼-volt dry battery issued with the NSPUM/1PN58 was also a carry-over item for 1PN51, which meant that the same portable battery charger could be used with either model.

In reality, the more advanced 1PN51 was granted its military GRAU Index Code at about the same time, or just prior to, the 1PN58, i.e., in the 1985 time frame. However, it did not enjoy widespread issue due to its higher expense (and limited production numbers) until 1989, when more efficient and inex-pensive methods of manufactur-ing its MCP components were perfected by engineers working under Orion.

The 1PN51 was exclusively manufactured at NPZ in Novo-sibirsk and served throughout the 1990s. It would eventually be adapted for issue with almost every infantry weapon in the Soviet arsenal, as well as the new Russian Federation. Rifles and other small arms mated to this sight were officially and specifically designated as AK74N-3, AKS74N-3, SVDN-3, RPK74N-3, RPKN-3, AKMN-3, SVDN-3, RPG-7N-3, PKN-3, VSS-ASS and AKS-74UN-3.

Both the 1PN51 and 1PN58 were manufactured and issued in tandem through much of their lifespan as part of a two-tier procurement system. Due in part to escalating costs and varying mission requirements, the Soviet military fielded two performance grades of NV optics simultaneously from 1985 onward, which allowed them to issue comparatively inexpensive, less advanced NV equipment to the majority of end-users while still acquiring (and financing R&D for) better-quality, higher-technology sights needed by more elite or important special-purpose units.

Throughout the 1990s, the new Russian Federation depended on both the 1PN51 and 1PN58 to soldier on as its primary small-arms night vision models. Both NPZ and Izhmash JSC marketed them to both military and new commercial customers as their primary NV equipment options for Kalashnikov applications. Today, these two types can still be found in limited service with secondary forces, although newer types are rapidly being procured, as finances permit, to replace them.

AN UNCERTAIN FUTURE

In the late 1980s, economic and political pressure forced a great many changes within the Soviet government as well as the Russian military-industrial complex that the Research Institute of Applied Physics (Orion) was a part of.

In 1989, the Soviet military was instructed to make a total withdrawal from Afghanistan, and by 1991 the Soviet Union collapsed entirely. For the next few years, the economic situation inside Russia made it impossible for larger military design and development projects to continue. In fact, the government was forced to shutter many production facilities as military contracts were frozen or severely limited.

Orion lost most of its research and production facilities and ties with other plants in places such as Belarus, Ukraine, the Baltic States and lower Asia. This drastically reduced its capabilities due to the loss of key resources, personnel and important manufacturing facilities.

It was not until 1994 that the Russian Federation realized the grave national security threat it was risking by letting this vital technological sector of its industrial base flounder. Therefore, in that year, it enacted a presidential decree that gave the Orion Corporation (as it was now democratically called) the status of the State Scientific Center. This would qualify it for needed government financial support and guarantee its survival. Thus, by the end of the decade, an entirely new line of second- and even third-generation night vision sights was ready for combat use by the reorganized military of the Russian Federation.

Many of the rifles seen in this article are painstakingly realistic recreated versions of Soviet firearms. We would like to thank these companies for their participation in this project:

This detail of the 1PN51 Kazuar displays the NPZ logo and military model nomenclature. This sight was the most advanced Soviet NVD available during the later years of the 1980s.

SOURCES

74U
Custom U.S.-made AK receivers
74ullc.com

Collector's Source DFW
AK optical mounting products
csdfw.weebly.com

Marshall Arms of Texas
AK building services
marshallarms.us

Scott Sandberg
Soviet militaria, posters and accessories

The classic I.O. AK-47C and an
accessorized, synthetic-stock
Hellhound, both in 7.62x39, are
now fixtures on the American
AK scene.

PHOTO BY MIKE ANSCHUETZ

THE ALL-AMERICAN AK

BY MARCO VOROBIEV

A FORMER SPETSNAZ SOLDIER REVIEWS A CROSS-SECTION OF OFF-THE-SHELF KALASHNIKOVS.

After the AK's initial inception in 1947, many were widely distributed to the USSR's "friendly" countries. Apart from guns themselves, the manufacturing licenses were also spread around. And AKs were manufactured in many countries without licenses. It is estimated that more than 70 million rifles have been produced and sold worldwide. Today, the civilian semiautomatic variants of the AK enjoy considerable popularity here in the U.S.

The AK's history in the U.S. is a tumultuous journey stretching from the very first Galil, Valmet and Type 56 variants to the current smorgasbord—a vast array of anything from collectible Tula and Izhevsk rifles to U.S.-made tactical carbines—and there are numerous reputable gunsmiths and custom shops that would gladly build a parts-kit rifle to your specification.

But what about off-the-shelf AKs? Whether they were imported, in kit form or fully U.S. built, I wanted to find out about them. Because I've been around AKs for a while, I had a few companies on my usual-suspects list. There are, in fact, many companies that import, convert or build AKs. Several do all three. I decided to concentrate my efforts on the most popular models in both 7.62x39mm and 5.45x39mm. With that in mind—and with a boatload of Wolf Performance ammunition (wolfammo.com) in both calibers—let's get started.

The AK74M in all its glory: The Arsenal's SGL31-94 is configured just like its military twin.

Arsenal's SGL21-61 is basically a sporterized version of the AK103 chambered in the original 7.62x39 caliber.

After more than 60 years in service with the Soviet and Russian armed forces, the AK continues to be a main battle rifle for Russia, former Soviet Republics and Eastern European countries.

ARSENAL

First on my list was Arsenal Inc. (arsenalinc.com). I picked Arsenal's most popular sellers, the SGL21-61 in 7.62mm and the SGL31-94 in 5.45mm. Both rifles start as AK103s and AK74Ms, respectively, at Izhmash Arsenal in Russia. Then, under the sporting label "Saiga," they are supplied to Arsenal. Arsenal then finishes them at its Las Vegas facility, bringing to the U.S. market the closest thing to the original Russian AK rifles ever offered.

SGL31-94 I wanted to take a closer look at the 5.45x39mm SGL31-94. There it was, the AK74M in all its glory. The rifle was equipped just like its military twin, with all the right Russian receiver and trunnion markings. It had a U.S.-made muzzlebrake, cleaning rod, side optics rail and black plastic furniture, with the exception of the Russian folding stock.

I fell in love with this folding-stock design back in 1985 during basic training and still consider it the best folding-stock solution for an AK. Unlike my old AK with its metal, skeletonized stock, the SGL31 comes with a solid plastic unit that includes a slot through its lower part for securing a recoil pad for use with a GP underbarrel grenade launcher.

7.62x39mm

5.45x39mm

Old and new, but both battle-proven: The original 7.62x39mm round and the 5.45x39mm.

The SGL31's package includes factory manual, test target and Izhmash 10-round magazine.

After stripping and reassembling it, I played around with shouldering, cycling and dry firing the rifle. The SGL worked very well through my exercises. It felt like a new AK should, bringing on a very familiar feeling. There was no drag on the bolt carrier, and the distinct double-stage trigger was nice and crisp. The finish was perfect, with that "new gun" appearance and feel. I set up prone at 100 yards, loaded it and started shooting.

There was minimal deviation between point of aim and point of impact. After 100 rounds or so, I was scoring consistent three-inch 10-shot groups, with the occasional flyer here and there. I was pretty content with the results, which exceeded the original Soviet accuracy requirements. The rifle did all this without a single hiccup. I used several magazines to see if the SGL31-94 functioned well with all of them. It did.

The I.O. Hellhound is a modern fighting carbine with a magazine-release tab that is slightly longer than that of the original AK.

The I.O. AK-47C is basically the classic AKM wearing laminate-wood furniture and a slant muzzlebrake/compensator. Its nonchromed barrel has the proper AKM-pattern gas block with bayonet lug.

SGL21-61 The SGL21-61 is basically a sporterized version of the current-issue Russian AK103 in the original 7.62x39 caliber with one exception—the fixed stock. As such, it had a very familiar configuration. The receiver bore the Russian arsenal proofmarks. The front trunnion also bore the "arrow in the triangle" Izhmash factory mark. The SGL21 was dressed in U.S.-made black plastic furniture. And just like its 5.45 sibling, it had a side mounting rail for attaching optics.

The original Russian chrome-lined barrel had a Russian front sight and gas blocks with bayonet and accessory lugs, and it was topped with Arsenal's U.S.-made AK74-style muzzlebrake. The finish of the rifle inside and out was impeccable, very close, if not identical, to that of Russian factory guns.

The SGL21-61 package contains a factory manual, test target and Bulgarian waffle five-round magazine. After stripping and reassembling it, I played around with it, shouldering, cycling and dry-firing. Operation was smooth, with no drag on the bolt carrier.

The SGL21-61 shot similarly well—the double-stage trigger was crisp, though recoil was more noticeable. If there had to be a surprise, I'd say it was the consistent three-inch groups at 100 yards, the same result I got from the 5.45mm SGL31. The SGL21-61 ate everything and asked for seconds. Not a glitch. No big surprise there. I was done with Arsenal rifles at this point. Both rifles shot very well and felt like AKs should.

INTERORDNANCE

Being involved in the U.S. AK scene for years, I am familiar

To the author's disappointment, there were no dimples on the GP-WASR receiver around the mag well. However, the correct Romanian side rail was in its usual place.

with I.O. Inc. (ioinc.us). The company's line of U.S.-built rifles includes the traditional, classically configured AK 47C laminated-wood model, based on the Russian AKM design, and more up-to-date models such as the STG 2000 and Hellhound.

I selected I.O.'s AK-47C Laminated Wood for its classic appeal and the Hellhound for its modern fighting-carbine features. Both are in 7.62x39. When the rifles arrived, they were nestled in the company's original packaging along with accessories. Both were built in North Carolina using U.S.-manufactured parts. Nonchromed barrels were installed into stamped U.S.-made receivers that sported side-mounted optics rails. Both rifles came with one 30-round polymer magazine, a cleaning-kit pouch, a sling and a manual. The finish on the rifles was a durable military type, but of a lesser quality than some of the more expensive AKs. Both of them proved to be solid shooters, well within AK performance parameters.

AK-47C This is the good ol' AKM in its original glory—laminate-wood furniture, slant muzzlebrake/compensator and nothing else that would violate the rifle's simple beauty. I couldn't help but immediately lift the AK-47C out of its box and shoulder it, as I've done thousands of times before. It felt so familiar that I neglected to notice the black plastic pistol grip, which added to the overall comfort. It was the only departure from a dead-stock AKM. It had the proper AKM-pattern front sight and gas block with bayonet lug.

I pulled the charging handle a few times and dry fired it before taking it apart. Once again there were no surprises. Everything was in its place, and all mechanisms functioned as expected. The weight, size and overall feel were unmistakably and quintessentially AK.

As expected, it shot exactly like an AKM. So I went to work to see what it could do on paper. Through magazine after magazine, I was scoring 4½-inch groups at 100 yards from prone. I was satisfied with the gun's performance. There were no malfunctions or stoppages. The I.O. plastic magazines functioned well, as did the rest of my test mags. Having all the attributes of a classic AKM, the AK-47C is a better shooter.

Hellhound While the AK-47C is pretty much a stock AKM rifle, the Hellhound is a departure from it. It has a slightly longer barrel topped with a YHM Phantom Flash Hider. The gas block is combined with the front sight, and there is no bayonet lug. The Hellhound sports quad Picatinny-rail handguards. It has the same black plastic pistol grip and Com Bloc-length plastic buttstock, resembling a "club foot" RPK stock. After shouldering the Hellhound several times, I found it very comfortable. The pistol grip/buttstock combination is well suited for it.

I pulled the charging handle a few times and dry fired it before taking it apart, finding it full of U.S.-made AK parts. Though at first glance the Hellhound appears drastically different, in reality it is still a good ol' AK. After reassembly, I loaded it, racked the charging handle and squeezed the trigger.

My first impression was, once more, a surprise. The Hellhound, equipped with a Phantom

The folding stock that came on the Tantal is a wire crutch-style right-side folder (above). The Century version featured a Bakelite lower handguard as opposed to the issue Polish version (top).

flash-hider, had noticeably increased recoil, even compared with the standard AKM slanted muzzlebrake. However, after my first magazine I got used to it and the difference faded away. The Hellhound ran smoothly throughout the test with no glitches. Though the quad Picatinny-rail handguard didn't offer an inherently comfortable grip, its practicality outweighs this minor inconvenience, one that is easily remedied by the addition of a small vertical grip. More than 100 rounds through the Hellhound produced consistent 3¾-inch groups.

CENTURY INTERNATIONAL ARMS

Century International Arms (centuryarms.com) offers a wide range of imported and U.S.-assembled and -built Kalashnikov variants, ranging from the Yugoslavian M76 Sniper to the Israeli Galani and its best-selling Romanian GP WASR-10. I picked the 7.62x39 WASR-10. Since I wanted to cover rifles in both main AK calibers, the other Century gun I selected was the 5.45mm-chambered Polish Tantal. The reason these rifles are on the list—and have contributed to Century's success—is the price.

Having tested several Century rifles in the past, I had no illusions when it came to its economically priced AKs. When I pulled both rifles out of their boxes, I couldn't help but crack a smile. Both were regular military infantry battle rifles, no more and no less. Crude around the edges with no shiny finish, these guns represent what the original AK-47 was intended to be—a mass-produced, simple, highly functional battle rifle. Both the Tantal and the GP WASR-10 are solid shooting machines—especially the Tantal. Aesthetically, they may concede a bit of ground to some of the other rifles, but this is easily remedied by replacing a couple of pieces of furniture.

GP WASR-10 The WASR appeared to be a basic AKM by look and feel. It came dressed in a combination of solid and laminate wood with a Tapco G2 trigger group, black polymer pistol grip, original slant muzzlebrake/compensator, bayonet lug, scope rail and, strangely, no cleaning rod. It did come with two Romanian steel 30-round magazines. When I cycled and dry fired it, it functioned as it should. The action was smooth enough, and the trigger felt pretty good.

As expected, the rifle wasn't shiny and possessed little glamour. It was a simple and functional AK that looked and felt like it. It looked crude in comparison with some of the guns I'd already shot. Then again, the WASR is not the type of gun you lay on your lap and gently stroke like a family pet. This is a gun you drag through mud, drop on concrete, pick up and expect to function. And function it did. It gobbled up everything I fed it out of a variety of mags without a single stoppage. It felt like the AKM-type rifle that it is. Shooting it prone, it produced 4½-inch groups at 100 yards all day. Every time I pulled the trigger it went bang.

Polish Tantal The Polish Tantal is a side folder and came equipped in its standard configuration, including all the Tantal-esque features, such as its original variation of an AK74-style muzzlebrake, Bakelite lower handguard, modified gas tube, plastic upper handguard and thumb safety, in addition to the regular AK lever. The folding stock is a wire crutch-style right-side folder seen on Romanian and East German rifles.

The Tantal came with two steel 30-round magazines, bipod and cleaning rod. Both bayonet and accessory lugs were present. I disassembled

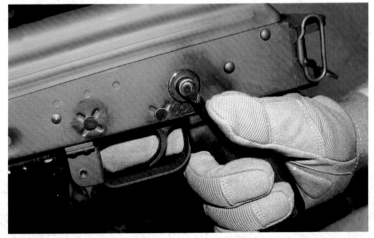

The SGL21's original Russian chrome-lined barrel was topped with Arsenal's U.S.-made AK74-style muzzlebrake.

and reassembled the rifle, then played around with it a bit, cycling the bolt carrier and dry firing it a few times. The operation was smooth and very AK-like. The single-stage Tapco G2 trigger group worked very well. Built by Century on the U.S.-made NoDak Spud receiver using an original Polish military parts kit and U.S. barrel, this gun was an enigma to me.

Being ultra-conservative, I didn't like what the Polish designers had done with my beloved AK74-type rifle. The weird muzzlebrake and wire stock only added fuel to the fire. With a mind full of prejudice, I shoved a mag into the gun, chambered a round and pulled the trigger. That first shot produced my first real surprise of the day. I actually had to stop and see whether the gun had in fact fired.

The recoil was so insignificant—even in comparison with

the SGL31-94—that I thought the Tantal had misfired. I pulled the trigger again and again, sending a round to my exact point of aim every time. The results were again very satisfactory, one 2¾-inch group after another. Handling characteristics and operation were superb. With its sharp edges, matte finish and rattling gas tube, it may be an ugly duckling, but it proved to be the best shooter of the day.

With a smile on my face, I put away the WASR and Tantal, and with that, I was done.

FINAL THOUGHTS

This article was not intended to compare several rifles with each other, but rather to describe what's available off the shelf and what is to be expected when selecting any of these. After my trips to the range, there were clear winners, but there were no losers. Each gun performed well, whether it was assembled or fully manufactured in the U.S. It all comes down to personal taste.

No matter what your new AK looks like, at least it's *still* an AK.

See some photos and specifications of the guns mentioned in this article and order from an inventory of thousands—all online through Gun Locator. Visit galleryofguns.com.

The thumb safety on the Tantal was only half-functional. Putting the safety on was almost effortless, but to take it off using the thumb lever proved impossible.

RUSSIAN AKMS. This is the underfolding-stock variant of the Soviet AKM. Chambered in 7.62x39mm, it is built on a stamped-steel receiver and has a metal underfolding stock based upon the German MP-40 submachine gun. It is fitted with a hammer-forged chrome-lined 16.1-inch barrel, laminated-wood furniture, synthetic pistol grip and slant-cut compensator. This particular rifle was built using parts Israel captured from the Palestinian Liberation Organization during the Lebanon conflict of the 1980s.

The Kalashnikov AK-47 and its variants are the most widely used military rifles in the world. It has been put into service by over 45 countries and seen action in every major military conflict since its creation in the late 1940s. While the overall design hasn't changed significantly, many countries added their own unique flavor to better fit their needs. In this article we will look at some of the most popular variants of the AK-47, and some of the lesser-known models as well. This guide can be used for identifying some of the less common models from around the world. The rifles pictured here are all semiautomatic clones owned by Kalashnikov Collectors Association member Stuart McDaniel.

POLISH PMKM. Chambered in 7.62x39mm, this is the closest clone of the Russian AKM in the world. It has a stamped-steel receiver, laminated-wood stock set, beavertail forend, synthetic pistol grip, slant-cut compensator and is pictured with a Polish bayonet and oil bottle.

POLISH PMKMS UNDERFOLDER. This is the stamped-steel-receiver version of the PMKM with underfolding stock. Chambered in 7.62x39mm, it has an AKM-type beavertail forend and a slant-cut compensator. It is pictured here with a Polish bayonet.

POLISH TANTAL WZ88. Chambered in 5.45x39mm, the Tantal is distinctive in that it features three-round-burst capability in addition to semi and auto. It also has a unique selector switch on the left side of the receiver (left). It is fitted with night sights and a distinctive muzzlebrake with a grenade launcher attachment. It also has Bakelite handguards and a side-folding metal stock that collapses to the right of the receiver.

ROMANIAN PM MD. 63. First produced in 1963, the PM md. 63 was Romania's first AK variant and was chambered in 7.62x39mm. It is almost identical to the Russian AKM, but has a chromium-plated bolt, chamber and piston. Also, it is fitted with an AK-47-style barrel nut and a wooden pistol grip.

ROMANIAN PM MD. 65.
The first underfolder from Romania, the PM md. 65 is identical to the original PM md. 63. Chambered in 7.62x39mm, it is built on a stamped-steel receiver and has a vertical foregrip.

ROMANIAN AIM-G. In 1989, Romania formed the 700,000-strong Patriotic Guard. They were equipped with semiauto-only PM md. 63 rifles that had a "G" engraved on the left side of the rear sight. This is the most popular version of the Romanian rifles, as over 20,000 of these rifles have been imported to the U.S. It is chambered in 7.62x39mm and fitted with a distinctive wooden vertical foregrip (left).

ROMANIAN AIMS 74. The 5.45x39mm variant of the PM md. 65, it has a vertical grip on the lower handguard and a sidefolding metal stock. The stock collapses to the right side of the receiver. An AK74-type muzzlebrake is fitted to reduce felt recoil.

YUGOSLAVIAN M92. Chambered in 7.62x39mm, this short-barrel AK has been used by Yugoslavian special forces. Built on a stamped-steel receiver, it has a two-position rear sight (inset) mounted to the top cover, underfold stock and

HUNGARIAN AMD-65.

Chambered in 7.62x39mm, this short, 12.6-inch-barrel rifle has the same foregrip as the AKM-63. A side-folding wire stock is fitted to make it more maneuverable in confined spaces, such as armored vehicles and tanks. The shorter sight radius and barrel make this a less accurate rifle than the AKM-63, but the added mobility offsets the loss in accuracy. Note the 20-round magazine.

YUGOSLAVIAN M70-B1.

Chambered in 7.62mm, this is the rifle that is issued to the Yugoslav army. Built on a heavier 1.5mm-thick RPK-type receiver, it has wooden furniture, rubber buttpad, gas shut-off valve and grenade-launcher sights. It can accept a thread-on grenade launcher. It is shown with an M52P3 anti-personnel land mine and some practice grenades.

HUNGARIAN AKM-63. First produced in 1963, the AKM-63 is a full-size rifle with a wood stock and a metal forend with a vertical wood foregrip to help control recoil during automatic fire. There is no upper handguard. Only about 1,100 of these were imported, so they are one of the rarest AK variants in the U.S. market.

EAST GERMAN MPI-KMS72. This sidefolder is chambered in 7.62x39mm and was produced at the Ernst Thaelman Factory in East Germany. With a wire stock, Bakelite grip and upper handguard, it was originally issued to airborne troops and mechanized infantry units.

CHINESE TYPE 56. The Chinese introduced a stamped-receiver variant of the Type 56 after China and the Soviet Union split. Because of this, the stamped-receiver model seen here was reverse-engineered without Soviet technical assistance. Two unique features of the Type 56 are the fully enclosed front sight and the folding bayonet cruciform. Also note the distinctive Chinese rivet pattern at the front of the receiver. It is estimated that 10 to 15 million Type 56 rifle have been produced since the 1950s.

CHINESE AK-47S. A semiauto version of the milled-receiver 7.62x39mm Type 56, it is the closest copy of the Russian AK-47 Type 3 that China ever made. Type 56 production was set up by the Soviets, who supplied machinery and technical assistance.

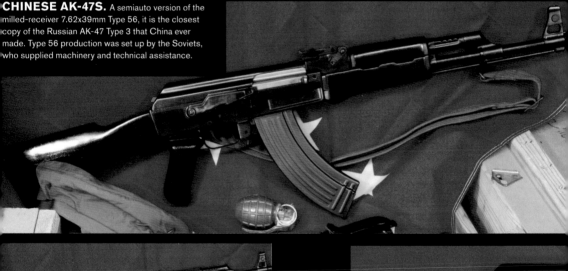

CHINESE AKS. Chambered in 7.62x39mm, this stamped-steel receiver AKS has a side-folding Phenolic stock set. It is one of the rarest of the Chinese guns in the U.S.

RUSSIAN AKM KHYBER PASS CLONE.
The Khyber Pass is the region between Pakistan and Afghanistan where the majority of trade routes are located. These rifles are normally made by gunsmiths in dirt-floored markets using whatever parts they can find. This rifle is chambered in 7.62x39mm and has an AKS-74-type side-folding stock. This is also the model that Osama bin Laden is seen shooting on several terrorist videos.

IRAQI TABUK CARBINE.
Chambered in 7.62x39mm, this Iraqi version was produced at the Al-Qadissiya establishments. Based on the Yugoslav M70B2, it has a stamped RPK-type receiver, wooden furniture, rubber buttpad, gas shut-off valve, rifle grenade launcher sight and a slant muzzlebrake. This model is capable of launching rifle grenades. A common sight in Iraq, many were captured by U.S. forces in Operation Iraqi Freedom and Operation Enduring Freedom.

EGYPTIAN ARM.
Chambered in 7.62x39mm, the "Maadi" (as some call it) was massively imported into the U.S. by Steyr-Daimler-Puch of New Jersey in the early 1980s. Built on a stamped receiver, the Maadi is a very close clone of the Russian AKM. This one has a side-folding wire stock.

This article would not have been possible without the generosity of Kalashnikov Collectors Association member, Stuart McDaniel. He graciously offered his impressive collection of rifles, memorabilia and knowledge for this article.

IRAQI TABUK DMR.
Chambered in 7.62x39mm, the semiauto-only Designated Marksman Rifle (DMR) version of the Iraqi Tabuk features a 23.6-inch barrel and a 4x24mm scope (Russian PSO-1 seen here, but Romanian LPS Type 2s and Yugoslav ZRAKs are also encountered) for engaging targets out to intermediate distances. It is often mistaken for the larger, more powerful 7.62x54R-chambered sniper rifles. It is essentially an accurized, scoped RPK.

PART II
STEP-BY-STEPS

BUILDING AN AK

Back to the future, mechanics-wise. | By Patrick Sweeney

The Romanian AK is one of the most common. You'll have to practice a bit to build one that looks (and is) this clean.

I have to admit right from the get-go that this is not really a "how-to-build" an AK-47, because that would take up the entire magazine you're holding. But rather this is a look at "how to avoid errors, mistakes and expensive dead-ends" in upgrading your Soviet blaster.

First of all, you have to understand that the AK was not designed to be modular. I'm not really sure the AR-15 was originally meant to be modular either, but since it has been driven by end-users and their checkbooks for the last 40 years, it has evolved that way. The AK-47 was meant to arm swarms of Soviet troopers, based on the experience the Red Army had in the Great Patriotic War.

To build an AK, you need three sets of parts: you need a receiver, a parts kit, and replacement U.S.-made parts. In reverse order, the U.S. parts are needed to make your rifle "922(r) compliant." That is, a lawfully assembled rifle. If you don't include enough U.S.-made parts, your rifle is in violation of the law.

The numbers are these: depending on the configuration of your particular AK parts kit, it has 15 or 16 parts on the import list. You can't have more than 10. So, you have to replace five or six with U.S.-made parts to be kosher. Since the U.S.-made parts aren't hard to find—and in many cases improve things (much better trigger parts, for one)—you'd be silly, even stupid, to avoid U.S. parts. Bonus: the receiver is a U.S.-made part, and counts towards the total. So before you even start, you're up by one. The main parts kit can be one of any of the many out there, although the supply has been getting scarcer. Why? My father has a saying, derived from his experience in the Great Depression and WWII: "Get yours before the hoarders do." For each of you cruising the aisles at gun shows, or scanning web pages looking for the perfect AK parts kit, there is some guy who bought his kits cheap and early,

The receiver, as-torched, leaves the trigger guard hanging out in space. As-shipped it is kind of delicate, so be careful in removing the rivets.

Here are two rivets—the upper one partially ground, and the lower one ground off flush with the sheet metal. Below: If you're lucky, they used a bandsaw to cut your parts kit up. The triggerguard is perfect here. However, this kit was covered in the nastiest, smelliest petrified petroleum product I've ever smelled.

You want the rivets ground off so you can remove the sheet metal receiver bits. Get the rivet heads off, but don't knarf the trunnions.

and has them stacked against the wall of his garage. They won't get cheaper; buy one or more. Buy them now.

The receiver is essential, and it is also unique. In the AR world, you can buy a receiver and build it up into any legal configuration or caliber. The same receiver could be a 5.56 shorty with a 16-inch barrel or a 6.8 DMR with a 20-inch barrel. Not so the AK. You must buy a receiver (or bend one—we'll get into that in a bit) that conforms to the parts kit. Is your parts kit a fixed-stock Romanian in 7.62? Then you need that receiver. You can't have a generic receiver, and decide "instead of the Romy 7.62, I'm going to build a 5.45 Tantal."

The AK just doesn't work that way. The bolt and ejector rails are caliber-specific, the magazine opening is caliber-specific, and the rear trunnion is stock-design specific. You also have to be aware of how many hooks your trigger system has. There are single-hook and double-hook setups, and each requires a slightly different opening for the trigger. Not that it matters much, but it can be a hassle, having to cut sheet metal to create clearance for your double-hook trigger on a single-hook lower.

If you order a receiver (it must go through an FFL holder; it is, after all a firearm) you must be specific. If you are not, you can count on the seller being unsympathetic to your plight. If you build one, you'll have to be specific, as not only will the seller be unsympathetic, but once bent or drilled, he can't take it back.

Receivers come in two forms: ready to build, or "80 percent" status. A ready-to-build receiver comes to you as a firearm; with holes drilled, rails welded, steel heat-treated and serial number applied. The 80 percent ones are either flats, which are just that: a flat section of steel with all the holes drilled, or they come as tubes with no holes created. Neither of them are firearms according to Federal law, but might be according to your state's laws. (Be sure and check before you go building an AK, or any other rifle.) With the flat, you must bend it into a channel, using a hydraulic press and holding fixtures. The tube requires that you glue a paper template to the tube, then drill and dremel all the holes.

It's The Law

Here's the interesting legal part: you can do this bending or drilling without an FFL. What you can't do, is do it as a business. *You* must do the actual bending and/or drilling. You cannot ask someone else to do the work for you. They are called "80 percent" receivers because someone

The top one is a firearm. The flat steel plate isn't, yet. As soon as you make the first bend, it is a firearm, and covered by all relevant state and federal laws.

Right: Here is an uncovered trunnion. Note that the rivets have been ground off and the sheet metal removed, but the trunnion itself is unharmed. This is the front trunnion, and next you'll need to remove the barrel pin and extract the barrel from the trunnion.

Single hook or double hook? It matters, but only a little. You can cut metal if you need, or leave a gap if you have to.

AKs do not have the adaptability of the AR. These four receivers can only be built as the type they were made for. The last one has some options, but those options mean a lot more work.

else has done less than 80 percent of the work to make it a firearm, and you must do the rest. In some locales, guys get together for "build" parties. They show up at a location, and help each other bending, drilling, assembling, etc. When it comes to bending flats, you must be the one pulling the handle on your flats. If your buddy bends the flats for you, he has just created his own receivers, not yours. (Even if you are standing there next to him, watching and helping.) Once bent, it is a receiver, *one that you cannot sell.* Build an AK from a flat, and you own it for life. (In a sympathetic administration, your heirs could probably inherit your home-built AK. And in a non-sympathic one, they won't. For now, no one really knows, as there have been too few of them inherited to matter.)

Whether you bend or drill, a digital calipers and a notebook are your friend. If you do not have the holding fixture precisely centered on your flat, or you do not have the template dead-evenly glued to your tube, you will ruin the potential AK receiver. "Close enough" doesn't count. If the holes don't line up, you've wasted your time, money and steel. Measure two or even three times, before you apply force of any kind.

Once you've built your 80-percent AK you can own, shoot, transport it, etc., like any other AK. The ATFE does suggest that you put some kind of serial number on it in case you need to identify it later, but they don't require it. Not only can you not sell it or give it away, some say you can't take it to a gunsmith. I don't see in the regs where it says that, but I will let you in on a dirty little secret of gunsmiths: some customers don't come back. Every gunsmith has a rack of abandoned firearms. The gunsmith can recoup his parts and labor expenses by requesting a mechanics lien, taking possession of the firearm, and then selling it to cover his costs. Your bent-flat AK? He can't do that. All he can do is turn it over to the ATF or police for disposal, and not get a penny for his efforts. That explains the resistance of gunsmiths to working on your AK. (That, and the cost/value ratio of homebuilt AKs is decidedly against him. Many customers are reluctant to invest in $100 of professional work on a rifle that might only be worth $200.)

The AK you built on a pre-bent, serial-numbered receiver? You can sell it if you wish, but be careful: If you build a bunch and keep most, then sell one to your brother, give one to the gunsmith who coached you, and donate one to the gun club for a raffle, no one will care much. But if you suddenly have a table full of AKs at the gun show, someone is going to

Don't be cheap. And don't be stupid. The easiest U.S.-made parts to get are the trigger system, which count as three of the five or six parts you'll need.

Rivets. I say again, rivets. Don't be tempted by the allure of screws of U-drives. Do it right, use rivets.

Yes, you can set many of the rivets with a modified bolt cutter. (This one has handles almost three feet long.) But there are some rivets you can't set with it, so you and your buddies should invest in a bucking bar.

This is your ejector. The ejector guides the bolt and throws the empties away. It has to be hard without being brittle. Take care to heat-treat it correctly, or you'll be disappointed.

wonder how you're in the business of making rifles, without a license. The ATF takes such things seriously, so don't make rifles to sell.

You face a few onerous tasks in building your rifle—first, getting the parts kit apart. Yours likely came as many of mine did, either caked in an awful, petrified, vaguely petroleum-based preservative, or as a collection of parts rattling around in a cardboard box. I had one kit that was coated in something so awful, I thought some critter had died in the shipping box. You need to fire up the bench grinder (or the hand grinder) and grind off the rivet heads of the receiver. What you want to do is extract the front and rear trunnions intact. The sheet metal of the receivers can get ground and scarred, who cares, you're going to pry it off with vise-grips anyway. (Those of you building with a milled-receiver kit, I pity you.) But the trunnions must be untouched.

You'll also have to exercise care to free the triggerguard without bending it. As-torched (that's how they were turned into parts kits) the triggerguard is an exposed and delicate thing. Be careful how you grind the rivets off.

Then you have to remove the barrel from the front trunnion. Unfortunately you can't fit the front trunnion to the new receiver with the

Inset: Learn what kind of rear trunnion your AK has. It will determine what kinds of stock options you can entertain. Below: Building isn't hard. But to build something like this (an SBR), you're going to need the tools, a kit, and a Federal Tax stamp. Know the law; don't go embarrassing us all.

You have to set these five rivets solidly, or your hand-built AK will not be happy. Get a bucking bar, and borrow time on a hydraulic press.

This is a 30-ton hydraulic press. You need it to bend flats and to set rivets. You need a lot of floor space for it, so borrow time on one.

barrel still in place. Those two rivets up top at the front? They have to be crimped into place with the barrel out, so you'll need a barrel press.

Even if you don't bend flats to make your own receiver, you'll need a bunch of tooling, and the place to get it is AGI (American Gunsmith Institute). You can also get detailed instructions on how all this goes from AGI. As I said, I could fill this entire publication with nothing but the instructions, additions and exceptions for how to build specific models of an AK.

Securing the receiver channel to the trunnions is a subject of controversy: The original method is done with rivets, hydraulically crimped to lock the parts together forever. Some will tell you that tapping the trunnions and using screws or bolts will serve as well, some advocate using U-drives, and I've seen photos of one AK that was welded together. (Shudder.) Avoid them.

Every gunsmith out there will tell you that parts should not be secured to firearms with screws. That manufacturers do it all the time (scope mounts being the biggest group here) does not make it right. Screws loosen under vibration. Scope mounts keep a scope in place (most of the time) but on your AK you're asking screws to be structural components of your assembly.

In designing the AK, Mikhail was told to make everything as cheaply as possible. And yet, some things aren't. In looking at the front and rear trunnions, I can see where there are several machine operations that could have been eliminated if economy trumped all other

Rivets are cheap. A whole set of good ones costs about a buck a rivet, so don't scrimp. And if you mess one up—extract it, buy a replacement, and do it right.

The top pin holds the barrel in place. The rivets secure the front trunnion to the receiver. If any are loose, your rifle will not work well, if at all.

considerations. So, obviously some quality or durability items defied the "make it cheap" dictum. If tapped and screwed fasteners sped up production, if it made the cost lower, if it made the receiver a part that could be overhauled, the Soviets would have done it. But rivets are all anyone has ever seen. Ever. That's validation enough for me.

Heat Treating

Your receiver must be heat-treated. The 100 percent-done, serial-numbered receiver that comes to your FFL holder is heat-treated. (At least it is if it is a good builder. There have been a few crappy AK receiver makers out there, and a quick web search will uncover their names.) However, your bent or tube receiver isn't. And you can't heat-treat the whole tube. You don't have the furnace and quenching tanks to do it properly. If you try to heat-treat the tube as a whole you'll either warp it, or get the temperatures wrong, and have a soft or brittle receiver. What you need to do is use a torch (MAPP works well) to heat the individual holes for the hammer and trigger. You can heat-treat the selector pivot holes if you want, but they don't need it. You do not want to heat-treat the river holes for the trunnions.

Heat-treating steel involves three steps: heat, quench and draw. You have to heat the holes one at a time to a bright yellow/orange color. Then dunk in ambient-temperature water. Some add salt, dish detergent or other agents to the water. Some use light oil. The differences are minuscule, and using oil is dangerous from the risk of fire. Once all the holes have been heated and quenched, they must be drawn, or annealed. At the quench hardness they are too hard. To draw them, brush the scale (that ugly, crusty stuff) off the receiver, and heat each hole to a dull purple and let air-cool. You're done.

Oh wait, there are the internal rails. They have to be hardened, or they won't last, either. Heat them to the same yellow-orange, and drop them in the quench oil. Once cool, fish them out and brush the scale off. Now, burning oil is your friend. Obviously, the next step has to be done out of doors on a calm day. (And not near a California forest!) Take a small metal dish, pour in an inch or so of light oil, add a light solvent, float the parts on top and light it. The oil will burn at the correct (or close-enough) temperature to draw the brittleness out of the rails. If you just can't bring yourself to burn them, then use the torch again to heat them to that dull purple. They have to stay dull purple for a couple of minutes, hence the burning-oil route.

Last are the rivets for the triggerguard. I'm assuming you haven't gone the screws, u-drive or welding route. You have to mushroom the rivet heads of the trigger guard. The cheap method of rivet-setting is to use a large set of cutters which have had the jaws modified to mushroom rivet heads. They work just fine on the trunnions, as there is room to reach. However, they are at best awkward, and at worst destructive, when used to set triggerguard rivets. It is crucial that these be set correctly and solidly.

The front of the triggerguard is also the magazine catch. If the rivets wobble, your magazines won't be properly positioned to feed well. You will be most unhappy with the result.

You really should look into something like the AGI "bucking bar." It locates and then mushrooms the heads of the bottom rivets all at once. To use it you need to have access to the hydraulic machine that you used to bend your flat, so no problem there. If you didn't bend a flat, then you're going to have to find someone who has a hydraulic press you can use for five minutes.

Unlike the situation with the AR-15, with which you can assemble a parts kit in a short time with a few hands tools (although the right tools do make it a lot easier) the AK, for all its simplicity, really requires good tools and a grasp of how it works. But you can do it. You just have to follow the old carpenter's adage: "measure twice, cut once." Except for setting rivets, you only get one chance to do each step correctly.

Think ahead; plan. Do it right.

SOURCE

American Gunsmith Institute
(800) 797-0867
www.americangunsmith.com

CRACKING THE AK
COMBINATION TOOL

A COMBO TOOL CAME WITH YOUR RIFLE, BUT DO YOU KNOW HOW TO USE IT?

BY **STEVE MILES**

Although AK cleaning kit/combo tools are common, many do not know how to properly use them or everything they can do.

Broken gas tube levers, bent front sight posts, deep scratches down the bore—these kinds of damage are not just seen on AKs in the third world.

Take a close look at AKs on the rack at your local pawn shop or on the table at a gun show, and you will see them as well. All are likely the result of using improper tools to maintain and adjust them.

"But it's an AK!" you shout. "There's nothing on that rifle a hammer, sickle and bottle of vodka can't fix."

While there is some truth to this sentiment, the fact is that each AK is issued with a well-thought-out combination tool. This is designed to simplify the more routine tasks and safeguard the rifle while being maintained by even the most ham-fisted conscript. While the AK combination tools themselves are very common, it is uncommon to find civilian AK operators who know many of the potential uses of the tool. This article will detail the purpose and function of the AK combination tool and its components as they were originally intended.

The combination tool is a capsule-like sheetmetal container, typically 93mm long, with either a black-painted or blued finish. The combination tool itself is composed of two-parts: the body and the cap. Located inside the combination tool are four to seven accessory tools. Every variant of the AK, however, seems to have its own unique combination tool. While some standardization can be seen in those issued with military AK rifles, versions of the rifle produced for the commercial market are often packaged with mismatched combination tools and accessories scrounged from surplus military production.

While the exact design and contents of combination tools will vary, the functions of the tool and its components are essentially the same. If your combination tool does not appear to work the way described below, or does not include the same accessory tools, in a pinch you can always fall back on the hammer, sickle and vodka expedient.

THE FINGER TRAP

In most wood- or polymer-stocked AK rifles the combination tool is commonly stored spring-loaded under a butt-plate trapdoor in the stock well. It is accessed by carefully inserting

Left to right: combination tool body, tool cap, bristle brush, screwdriver blade, drift and patch loop from a Saiga IZ-132 7.62x39mm rifle.

a finger into the trapdoor and applying pressure on the combination tool until it comes out of the well under the pressure of its spring. More than a few comrades have pressed their finger in too far and become snared by the trapdoor as they attempt to withdraw their digit from the stock well. This is sort of a less painful Russian version of "M1 thumb." On other AK rifles, the combination tool is safely stored in an accessory pouch, usually with an oil bottle and spare magazines.

DESCRIPTIONS AND FUNCTIONS

Combination tool body: The body is a storage tube perforated with various slots and oval holes. The combination tube body is used as a cleaning rod handle, screwdriver handle, front sight post adjustment-tool handle and for rotating the gas-tube locking lever. When using the combination tool body as a cleaning-rod handle, first insert the nonthreaded end of the cleaning-rod end into the large slot on the side of the tool body, then insert the screwdriver blade through the open end of the tool

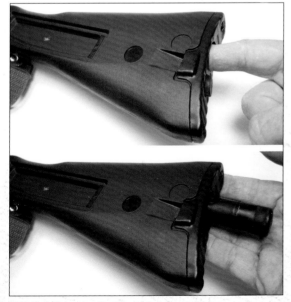

Combination tool being removed from the spring-loaded trap of a Russian AK100-series rifle.

Many Com-Bloc magazine pouches, like this one for a Polish PMKMS underfolder, have pockets for the combination tool.

One slot in the combination tool body is for rotating the gas-tube locking lever.

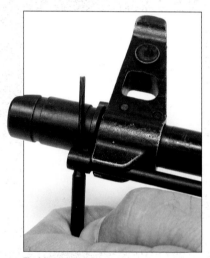

The drift can be used to remove the cleaning rod from the rifle more easily.

body to secure the cleaning rod in the handle. When using the combination tool body to rotate the gas-tube locking lever, fit the narrow slot running lengthwise on the closed end of the tool body to the tab on the locking lever.

DRIFT: The drift is a 75mm-long shaft tapering from 4.7mm to 1.9mm in diameter. It is suitable for light impact work with a small hammer or other field expedient. The drift may be used to assist removal of the cleaning rod from the rifle by inserting the drift through the hole on the nonthreaded end of the cleaning rod. The drift may also be used to remove a stuck combination tool cap by inserting the drift through holes on both sides of the tool cap and rotating. When disassembling the fire control group, the drift may be used to tap out the axis pins. Prior to removing the hammer, the drift should be used to lift and secure the hammer spring legs behind the hammer sear. The drift is also the primary tool for disassembling the bolt using the following four steps:

1. Drive out the pin that retains the firing and extractor pins.
2. Remove the firing pin.
3. Drive out the extractor pin.
4. Remove the extractor and spring.

SCREWDRIVER BLADE: The screwdriver blade has two functional ends. One is a flat 7mm-wide standard screwdriver bit tapering to a near-chisel point. This end can be used to tighten or remove the screws found on the butt plate and stock screws, as well as the pistol-grip bolt. The other end has a slot and hole for use as a wrench and sight-adjustment tool. On some versions there is a notch cutout on one side of the blade that can be used as a wrench to tighten or loosen the bristle brush, jag or patch loop when threaded onto the cleaning rod. For additional leverage when turning or prying, the screwdriver blade should be inserted into the side slots of the combination tool body, passing through both sides.

The screwdriver blade is likely the most versatile of the accessory tools. The slotted end of the screwdriver blade can be used to adjust elevation on the front sight post. When viewed from the top, turning clockwise moves the point of impact up; counterclockwise, down. The flat end may be used to pry the lower handguard retainer locking lever open, as well as tighten or remove the pistol-grip bolt, stock screws and butt-plate screws.

PATCH LOOP OR JAG: AK combination tools usually contain either a patch loop or jag. Both are accessory tools used for cleaning and

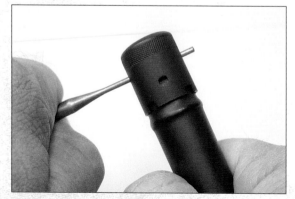

The drift can be utilized to remove a tight cap from the combination tool body.

The drift can be used to lift the hammer spring legs prior to removal of the hammer.

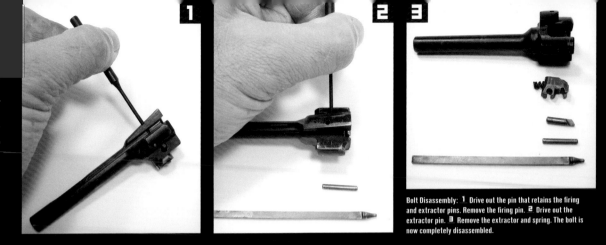

Bolt Disassembly: **1** Drive out the pin that retains the firing and extractor pins. Remove the firing pin. **2** Drive out the extractor pin. **3** Remove the extractor and spring. The bolt is now completely disassembled.

lubricating the rifle barrel bore and other components by use of an affixed cloth patch. Rifles with a jag will typically have a cleaning rod with a slot for a patch.

COMBINATION TOOL CAP: The smaller part of the combination tool is the cap, which has pressed lugs and may be perforated with various holes. The combination tool cap may be used as a bore guide on some AK rifles.

CLEANING THE BARREL

One of the most potentially damag-ing tasks when maintaining an AK is cleaning the barrel. This is due to the fact that one must clean the weapon from the muzzle, rather than the breech, with the issue rod. When used properly, the steel cleaning rod and tools will keep your rifle well maintained. When used improperly, they can easily nick the barrel crown. This can cause an immediate degradation in accuracy or lead to chrome flaking and future accuracy problems. Improper cleaning from the muzzle, with the rod not properly centered in the bore, can also wear the crown over time. To avoid this damage, the issued cleaning rod and tools should be configured as follows:

1. Insert the nonthreaded end of the cleaning rod into the largest side slot of the combination tool body.
2. Insert the screwdriver blade into the combination tool body, thereby locking the cleaning rod in place.
3. Slide the combination tool cap onto the cleaning rod with the cap opening toward the threaded end of the cleaning rod.
4. Screw the bristle brush, jag or patch loop onto the cleaning rod.

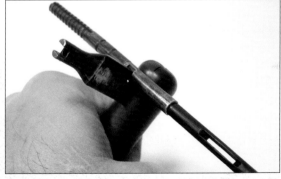

Using the wrench notch on the side of the screwdriver blade can tighten or loosen the jag on the cleaning rod. Note the patch slot on the cleaning rod.

By placing the front sight tool into a slot in the combo tool body, you can adjust eleva-tion on the front sight post. When viewed from the top, turning clockwise moves the point of impact up; counterclockwise, down.

The AK only has a few screws, but the screwdriver blade can be used to tighten or remove them.

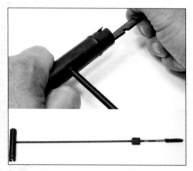

The combination tool body, screwdriver blade, cleaning rod, tool cap and bristle brush are configured for proper barrel cleaning.

When configured in the above manner the combination-tool cap will act as a bore guide and keep the steel cleaning rod away from the easily damaged muzzle walls and crown. The combination tool cap has pressed lugs that will engage slots on a slant brake or muzzle nut to hold the cap securely in place during cleaning. The drift can be used for leverage should the combination tool cap become jammed on the slant brake or muzzle nut.

Cleaning the barrel bore from the

SOURCE

The Official Soviet AKM Manual
Paladin Press, 1998

muzzle end with a steel cleaning rod is the protocol found in old Soviet AK operator manuals, but there are safer methods available today. The use of a longer cleaning rod from the chamber end is less likely to cause damage. Also, using a cleaning rod made from soft metal, carbon fiber or one that is powdercoated can reduce risk to the barrel bore when cleaning, if you keep the rod clean. A simple cord pull-through is cheap and effective. It may be best to restrict the use of the steel AK cleaning rod to field use where other rods are not available or when obstructions must be removed from the bore.

ONE TOOL, MANY USES

The AK rifle is very capable when employed as intended. So, too, is the AK combination tool. The combination tool fills the roles of many other items and at the same time reduces the risk of damage when maintaining and adjusting the AK. While this article has recounted the uses of the combination tool as they would have been explained to a Soviet conscript, an enterprising AK operator can find even more uses for this versatile implement.

Acknowledgement is due to Major James F. Gebhardt, U.S. Army (Ret.), for his invaluable work translating and publishing the ex-soviet AKM operator's manual that was used while researching this article.

Press and rotate the combination tool cap to secure it to the slant brake or muzzle nut. This serves as a bore guide to prevent the steel rod from damaging the crown. The Soviet manual says to remove the brake/muzzle nut if the rifle has been fired extensively.

The drift can be used for leverage should the combination tool cap become jammed on the slant brake or muzzle nut.

The AK combination tool is also useful once your rifle has been cleaned. Here it's used to open a cold, post-range beverage.

AN AK FRONT SIGHT TOOL EVERYONE SHOULD TAKE TO THE FIELD.

I f you own an AK-type rifle, you will probably have to zero it. Zeroing is primarily accomplished through adjustment of the front sight. A little field-expedient tool is provided in the buttstock cleaning kit for adjusting elevation, and inexpensive commercial tools that resemble a C-clamp are available for adjusting windage and elevation. You may be able to get by with average tools in most cases, but then again, the day may come when you're trying to adjust the rusty windage drum on a rifle your buddy built from a $99 parts kit and you start thinking about torches and hammers because the damned thing won't budge.

Sounds like you need the mother of all sight tools, from Magna-Matic Defense. Actually, it's called the AKFST, which stands for AK Front Sight Tool. Made from zinc-plated solid steel in the U.S., it's advertised as 400 percent stronger than conventional C-clamp-type tools and carries a lifetime warranty. One look at it and you won't doubt the claims of strength. The main body of the AKFST fully encircles the front sight tower during windage adjustments, and the long, stainless steel adjusting arm provides plenty of torque. The elevation adjustment wrench fit snugly over the Romanian, Bulgarian and Hungarian front sights I had on hand, and in fact, a tap was required to seat it on all three. As impressed as I was with the AKFST, I was surprised to learn that an even heavier-duty "gunsmith" model, the AKFST-GS, is now available and claims to be 900 percent stronger than the C-clamp tools. View these high-quality products at magna-matic-defense.com.

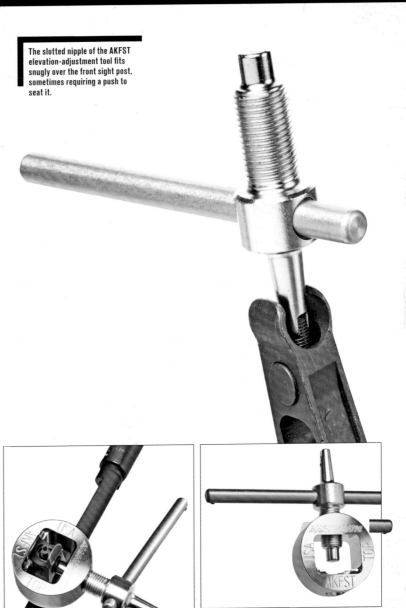

The slotted nipple of the AKFST elevation-adjustment tool fits snugly over the front sight post, sometimes requiring a push to seat it.

The AKFST fully encircles the front sight housing, and the long handle provides plenty of torque.

BY GUS NORCROSS

1

Flip the sight up to vertical and look straight down at it. You will see the tip of the leaf spring protruding from under the front of the sight leaf. Behind the sight you will see two slots cut into the sight housing for installation and removal of the leaf. The goal here is to push the spring down far enough to align the sight studs with the slots and allow the sight to be pulled rearward and out of the housing.

2

Insert the screwdriver into the slot in front of the sight and push down on the tip of the leaf spring. The spring may not move easily, so get a solid position over the rifle and try not to slip and cut your hand on the sight leaf.

3

Once the tension is removed from under the sight leaf, you can pull it rearward and out of the housing.

R emoval of the AK-47 rear sight is not usually necessary, but if you deal with these rifles as an armorer, sooner or later you will have to remove one for replacement or refinishing. This is a simple task, accomplished in the following steps with or without a special tool.

The only tool required is a simple flat-tip screwdriver. The sight is under considerable tension from the stout leaf spring that holds it in place, so you will want the rifle solidly clamped in a padded vise. Remove the handguards so the vise will grip directly on the rear sight housing.

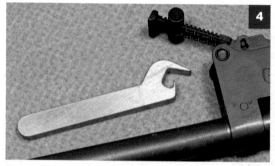

4

Removal of a rear sight in the field without a vise can be tricky. You will need someone to hold the rifle steady while you push on the sight leaf, or you can purchase one of these cool sight leaf tools from Power Custom.

5

Flip the sight forward and insert the tip of the sight tool under the leaf while hooking the claw under the edge of the sight housing and levering the tool handle up to push down the leaf. It's very simple and painless once you try it. The tool is available through Brownells (brownells.com/Part# 713-000-121).

ARMORER

Disassembly of the AK-47 bolt is very simple. The only tools needed are a small 1/16-inch punch and a hammer for tapping out the extractor and firing pin retainer pins.

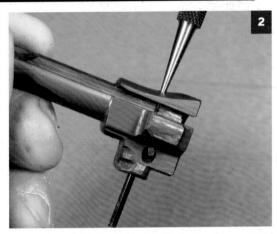

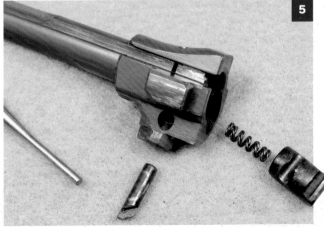

1. Look at the bottom of the bolt and locate the hole for the firing-pin retaining pin between the locking lugs.

2. Punch out the firing-pin retaining pin with the 1/16-inch punch. You might have to tap it with the hammer to get it moving. This pin passes through a notch in the extractor pin.

3. Remove the firing pin out of the rear of the bolt. Some firing pins are flat-sided, and some are round with flutes, but all of them will have a clearance cut for the retaining pin near the tip. This notch must be oriented correctly on reassembly.

4. Locate the extractor pin on the bolt bottom.

5. Push the extractor toward the bolt face to ease pressure on the pin and push out the pin. Release the extractor and remove it and the spring. Note the rear groove in the extractor that the pin passes through to retain it.

ZEROING THE AK-47

A step-by-step guide to sighting-in your AK by the Soviet textbook.

By James Tarr

Getting the most from any rifle, AK included, requires a good zero. The Soviets had a set pattern for ensuring it was done properly.

Our family has dinner together most every night. While I have a job so I can put food on the table, and gas in the Hemi-powered SUV, my number-one responsibility is raising my two sons. That's with the help of my wife, of course. Part of that responsibility is doing my best to make sure my sons are well spoken and well read. So I do not shy away from using "big" words during conversation. Unfortunately (or perhaps not), my boys frequently ask, upon hearing such words, "What's that mean?" More often than not I find myself saying, "Umm, well...here, let me get the dictionary and I'll read you the definition." The most recent instance of my mouth outrunning my brain involved the word "ubiquitous." Webster defines ubiquitous as "present everywhere; being everywhere, esp. at the same time; omnipresent."

I used the word "ubiquitous" to describe the AK-47, and while I was a little fuzzy on the exact wordage, I had the general definition right. If there is any weapon that is more omnipresent in the world than the AK-47 (and its variations), I don't know what it would be. The Avtomat Kalashnikova was designed

The Official Soviet AKM Manual, available through Paladin Press, is an invaluable resource for the care, feeding and zeroing of the ubiquitous rifle.

more than 60 years ago and has been made in the Soviet Union, most of its Eastern European satellites, China and at least 16 other countries at last count. Nearly 50 countries issue the AK as their military arm. People have earned Ph.Ds studying subjects less complex than the family tree of the AK-47. My boys (one of whom is 6) know what an AK-47 looks

like, not because we live in a Third World dictatorship (although I do work in Detroit occasionally), but instead because they play video games. And nothing else looks like it. Whether they have fixed stocks or folders, either underneath or to the side, or are chambered in the original 7.62x39mm or newer 5.45x39mm, all AKs are nearly identical in operation and very distinctive in appearance.

American soldiers are once again in conflict with an enemy armed with the ubiquitous AK. Accounts of our grunts using seized AKs to defend themselves, because their own rifles either jammed or ran out of ammo, are numerous. Gunsite, the U.S. Shooting Academy and many other firearms training facilities offer courses to U.S. soldiers to familiarize them with the weapons of the enemy. Knowing how to operate the AK laying on the ground in front of you when your M4 seizes up is something every U.S. soldier should know. Knowing how to zero that AK when the dust has settled is just as important, considering how many AKs are in U.S. stores in Iraq and Afghanistran.

The basic design of the AK is 60 years old, and Mikhail Kalashnikov was more interested in creating a reliable rifle than

Left: This steel-case Russian ammo, sealed and coated with lacquer to protect it, is exactly what the doctor ordered for inclement weather use with the AK-47. The AK design is so simple, even used and battered-looking magazines tend to work well.

A Chinese semiauto version of the Type 56 was used for this article. Michigan in December isn't quite as challenging as Siberia, and AKs can handle snow as well as they can sand.

The AK-47 front sight post can be accessed from the front, rear and top. One rotation of the front sight post will change the point of impact 20 cm (approximately eight inches) at 100 meters. The rear sight set at 300 meters per the Russian "Old Method" of zeroing an AK-47.

one with tackdriving accuracy. Gaston Glock had the same idea. This is why I can read a newspaper through the gap between the slide and frame in my Glock 34, but it goes bang every time I pull the trigger. The AK has the same reputation that the M1911 .45 used to. Namely, that it was reliable, but horribly inaccurate. In the case of those .45s, most of those pistols suffered from age and neglect and were relatively inaccurate, as far as pistols go. But the design itself, as we all know, is not inherently inaccurate. The same is not exactly true for the AK family of firearms.

Manufacturing tolerances, or the lack thereof, are as responsible for AK inaccuracy as anything. These loose tolerances were designed into the weapon to allow it to work even after being buried in sand or frozen solid. Compounding the problem is the fact that many of these

rifles are being built on machinery as old as the design itself abd in places where you'd be foolish to drink the water.

The original Official Soviet AKM Manual issued by the Ministry of Defense of the USSR, a copy of which I obtained from Paladin Press, is a must for any AK owner. It states that a "normal" four-shot group, when sighting-in at 100 meters, should be 15 cm or smaller in diameter. That's six inches, folks. Not exactly benchrest-level accuracy. But even with that worst-case scenario, an issue AK is more than accurate enough to hit a man-size target out beyond 200 yards— providing it's properly zeroed and the shooter is doing his job.

In researching the proper way to zero a 7.62x39mm AK-47, I discovered two different methods. The first I'll cover is the by-the-book Soviet military method.

Old Official Soviet Procedure:

1. Place a confirmation target at 100 meters (109.4 yards) with a spot or edge you can aim at precisely. The control point, or required point of impact, shall be 25 cm (approximately 10 inches) above the point of aim.

2. Set the rear sight at 300 meters. Set the rifle for semiautomatic fire.

3. From the prone position, with the forearm supported on a sandbag, fire four aimed shots at the center of the bottom edge of the black portion of the confirmation target. Do not move or break the cheekweld between shots.

4. The group shall be no larger than 15 cm (5.9 inches). One called flier is permitted, optionally.

5. The center of the group shall be no farther than 5 cm (1.97 inches) from the control point. If the group is not within this distance, adjust the sights and repeat until the center of the group is within 5 cm of the control point.

6. Set the rear sight at 100 meters. The rifle is now zeroed.

The Soviets issued a specific target for zeroing in this manner, and it is important to use a target of these dimensions for best results. It consists of a black rectangle 35 centimeters high by 25 centimeters wide (14x10 inches) centered in a white background one meter high by a half-meter wide (39.3x19.6 inches). The aiming point is the middle of the lower edge of the black rectangle. This target is specifically sized for the width of the AK front sight at this distance and provides enough contrast for easy sighting. The reasoning behind having the Point of Impact (POI) 10 inches above the Point of Aim (POA),

Zeroing an AK-47. Use a rest for the forearm whenever possible, as opposed to resting the weapon on the magazine.

with the sights set at 300 meters, is to match the trajectory of standard M43 ball ammunition. The result is a true 300-meter zero. By placing the rear sight on 100 meters, POI should now be the same as POA at 100 meters.

New Method:

This method seems to have been developed in the U.S. to simplify zeroing, especially for those locations where 100-meter ranges were not available:

1. Set the rear sight at 100 meters and the sight-in target at 25 meters (82 ft.).

2. Sight-in so the bullets are hitting exactly to point of aim. With that, the rifle is sighted for any range.

3. After sighting in, if you set the sight on the Battle Sight setting (the lowest on the sight scale) you can hit a man-size target at any range from zero to 400 meters without changing the sight setting.

The problem with this method is that it does not take into account cumulative error in the tangent rear sight. Although it works well for short-range use, a rifleman using this method may find considerable error in his POI when firing at extended distances. Due to this, this method is best reserved for when you only have a 25-meter range available.

Adjusting the Sights

The AK's front sight is screwed into a round steel piece that is set sideways into the triangular front sight base. Windage adjustments are made by drifting the block left or right. Numerous companies make an AK-47 front sight adjustment tool, which acts like a C-clamp with a screw to adjust windage. This is a handy item to have, but it's not absolutely required; a field-expedient method, otherwise known as a hammer and an empty cartridge case, will suffice. Place the spent case on the round sight base and tap gently, because one millimeter of lateral movement will adjust the point of impact 26 cm (approximately 10 inches) at 100 meters.

Elevation adjustments are made by screwing the front sight in and out. A front sight tool specifically made for this purpose is included in the cleaning kit normally stored in the rifle's butt trap. One complete revolution of the front sight will move the point of impact 20 cm (approximately eight inches) at 100 meters. Screw it down and the point of impact goes up; move the front sight up and the point of impact goes down.

While I first fired an AK-47 back when Reagan was president, the past few years I've spent most of my tactical long-gun time on the M4. My first thought upon

The field-expedient method of adjusting the front sight for windage: a hammer and a spent cartridge case. Right: The first group fired after adjusting the sights to hit the prescribed Control Point. POI is a point approximately 25 cm from the POA at the bottom of the black target rectangle.

picking up an AK was, "What a dinosaur." AKs look like they were designed in the 1940s. They're heavy and blocky, and many models sport wood furniture not seen on military arms anymore. Well, guess what—they were designed in the 1940s. That said, in many ways it's a very ergonomic design. It balances well, the pistol grip puts the finger on the trigger in just the right spot, and the buttstock is short enough to use while wearing body armor.

For this article I used a ubiquitous (there's that word again) Chinese-made Norinco Type 56 with a stamped receiver. This one happens to have an excellent trigger, which broke at just under four pounds. With no stacking and a surprise break, this trigger helped immensely when we were zeroing the rifle. While most of our soldiers currently in harm's way see more sand than snow, the AK-47 was designed in the country that gave us Siberia. So I had no problems when zeroing the rifle in Michigan with several inches of snow on the ground. At least, no

A dedicated front sight tool that can adjust both windage and elevation is handy to have and makes zeroing much quicker.

problems with the rifle—hands and feet and noses were another matter. I could have used a nice Russian sable fur hat.

When zeroing the rifle using the official Soviet method, I decided to go "old school." For a rifle rest I used a half-frozen sandbag, cradling the forearm in my gloved hand. Test firing was done in weather Muscovites would find positively balmy, and I hardly felt the cold under my five alternating layers of cotton, wool and polar fleece. Ammo was steel-cased Russian 7.62x39mm with red sealant around the case mouth and primer to help keep out the elements.

The sub-four-pound trigger on the test gun helped to keep the sights on target during sighting in. But with less than a tight grip on the gun I discovered it was possible to float the trigger. Two-round bursts can be exciting when you're not expecting them.

Premature-ignition issues aside, I can't think of a target that would work better for zeroing an AK than the old official Soviet one. At 100 meters, the 35x25-cm (14x10-inch) rectangle was the exact same size and shape as the front sight post. Lining up the top of the front sight with the bottom of the sighting rectangle is a very natural thing to do. Plus, with the prescribed white background, any movement off center immediately reveals itself.

Using the Russian steel-cased ammo, the test gun was capable of sub-five-inch groups at 100 meters. That's good enough to hit a man in the chest at 300 meters, which is what this rifle was designed for. Properly zeroing an AK, such as outlined here, will allow a rifleman to get the most out of it. If you are looking for a zeroing method for your AK, consider how the Russians teach it. They have been using them longer than anyone, and they know a thing or two about it.

DISASSEMBLY OF THE AK FIRE CONTROL GROUP.

BY **GUS NORCROSS**

2. Look up through the magazine well, and locate the hooked end of the shepherd's crook.

3. Take your hooked scribe or a pair of needle-nose pliers, and give the hook a yank toward the muzzle. It should pull free and will probably end up across the room under a bench. Don't worry about it. We're not going to use it again.

If you own an AK, it only makes sense to know it inside and out. This includes being able to remove/install the fire control components. Follow along, and learn how.

Removal of the fire control parts of AK-type rifles is not normally necessary during routine maintenance. However, if you are building a rifle or replacing the trigger group with aftermarket parts for better performance, this tutorial may prove useful. A U.S.-made fire control group counts as three of the six required compliance parts when assembling a rifle from an imported parts kit.

Clear the rifle and fieldstrip it. The only tools you will need are a punch to push out the trigger and hammer pins, and a scribe with one end shaped like a hook. You might also need the slave pin from the issued AK buttstock cleaning kit, depending on which model trigger you are installing.

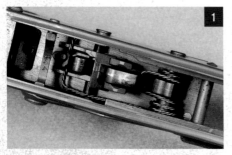

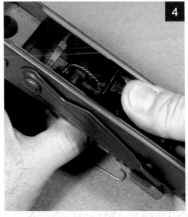

1. Take a good look at how the fire control components are assembled in the receiver. Starting at the rear is the safety. When you flip up the lever, it blocks the trigger. Forward of the safety is the trigger/disconnector assembly, followed by the hammer. The hammer spring is made of twisted-coil wire that wraps around the hammer with two extended prongs resting on the trigger. On the left side of the receiver is a piece of wire running under the trigger pin, over the hammer pin and under the receiver center support ending in a hook. This is the pin retaining spring, sometimes referred to as a shepherd's crook, among other things.

4. Grasp the receiver so you can put your thumb on the hammer to control it. Push the hammer down slightly, pull the trigger with your other hand, and let the hammer go forward.

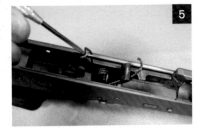

5, 6. Take the hooked end of your scribe, and pull the ends of the hammer spring forward so they are retained on the front of the hammer.

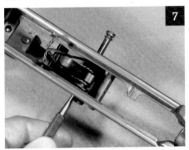

7. Push out the trigger pin with your punch. The disconnector and spring may pop loose as the pin is removed. Remove the trigger. Push out the hammer pin. You will have to slide the hammer to the rear to lift it out of the receiver with its spring.

8. Turn the safety lever so it points straight up, and pull it out of the receiver. On some rifles you may remove the safety lever at the beginning of disassembly, and on some you have to remove the trigger first. It all depends on the parts mix in your rifle.

9. Fire control components disassembled. Note the grooves in the heads of the pins for the retainer spring. These pins are interchangeable, so don't worry about mixing them up.

10. Two types of triggers you may encounter. The trigger on the left is disassembled, showing the three parts: trigger, disconnector and disconnector spring. These parts are retained in the rifle solely by the trigger pin and will separate during disassembly. To simplify reassembly, a slave pin is supplied in the standard-issue cleaning kit, so these parts may be joined as a subassembly when placed in the receiver. The trigger pin pushes out the slave pin as it is inserted. The trigger on the right is the popular Tapco G2 assembly. This trigger comes assembled on a sleeve, so it is removed and replaced as one assembly.

11. The pin retainer spring locks into the grooves in the heads of the trigger and hammer pins to prevent them from vibrating loose while firing the rifle, which would disable it. While the AK-47 is, for the most part, a robust rifle, this part is unfortunately a weak point. It's a pain to remove, it's a pain to install, and it's prone to failure. I advise replacing it with a sheetmetal retainer and never looking back. The part in the photo was developed by Marc Krebs of Krebs Custom, one of the most knowledgeable AK builders in the country, to replace the bent paper clip that holds your AK together. Ten bucks. Get one.

12. It is wise to tie up the ends of the hammer spring so they can't snap out of place and produce puncture wounds in your hand as you're replacing the hammer. It's very uncool to bleed all over your AK. A piece of string, a rubber band, tape, a plastic zip tie or anything similar will work. Before you slide the hammer into the receiver, note that one of the holes is countersunk for the head of the hammer pin. This countersunk hole should be on the left side as you slide the hammer into the receiver. The hammer will not go in backward. Ask me how I know.

13. This photo shows the orientation of the Krebs retainer plate to the hammer and trigger pins. Reinstall the hammer and hammer pin and then the trigger and trigger pin. The open end of the plate slides into the groove in the head of the hammer pin. Then rotate the plate downward so the notch in the middle locks the trigger pin in place. Everything is solidly locked in place when the safety lever passes through the hole at the rear. Using your hooked tool, release the hammer spring ends, and position them back in place on the trigger. Cock the hammer, and reassemble the rifle.

PART III
GEAR AND ACCESSORIES

AK FOREARMS

THE standard forearm on an AK is utilitarian. Then again, the whole rifle is, really. But that doesn't stop users and designers from coming up with useful replacements, semi-useful replacements and downright useless ones too. After all, comrade, this is a consumer-driven economy. If enough people want an AK with furniture in Barney purple, someone will make it. (I shuddered as I wrote that.)

When the AK-47 was being developed, no one mounted lights on a rifle. No one knew what a laser was, outside of readers of science fiction. As for making a place on a rifle to mount them, get serious, comrade.

The main problem with a railed handguard on the AK is how to attach it. Before we delve into handguards, let's look over the engineering of it all. You'll need to know this, to install yours.

On most AKs, the handguard is laminated wood, and is lacking a heat shield. Some of the AK74 models have a heat shield, but not all do. Unload and show clear, then remove the top cover, carrier and bolt. Now go to the side of the rear sight tower. There's a lever there. That lever locks the piston tube in place. Rotate the lever up. You may have to exert a bunch of force to do that, as they are not meant to be easily dismantled. Once you rotate the lever far enough it frees the rear of the tube, which you can lift clear.

Now look at the right front of the lower handguard. (Those of you with the Stg-2000 Weiger derivative rifles are out of luck. No replacement handguards will fit.) There is a lever there, one you'll have to pry with a

screwdriver. It will not move with your bare fingers, unless one of two conditions exists: it is so loose it rattles, or your hand strength rivals that of a set of vice-grips. Once pried up, you can move the front retainer assembly forward on the barrel, and then remove the current handguard.

A quick perusal of the system will quickly show you that there is no such thing as a "free-float" rail system. Everything attached to your Kalashnikov bears on the AK barrel, so you won't get any joy there. On the AR, a free-float handguard removes pressure and stress on the barrel, and can improve accuracy. That approach isn't possible on the AK. Even if you could free-float the barrel, you'd still have the gas tube and piston banging on it. The handguard, old or new, is going to be trapped between the receiver face and the front assembly. If it is too tight, it will have an effect on accuracy. (Not that anyone will notice.) If too loose, it will rattle and shift.

The new railed lower simply (well, not always "simply" but sometimes that is life) fits back in place

This experienced contractor finds that the CAA handguards work just fine for him. Hard to argue with experience.

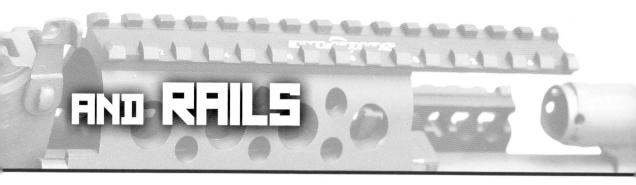

AND RAILS

When you really have to have lots of stuff | By Patrick Sweeney

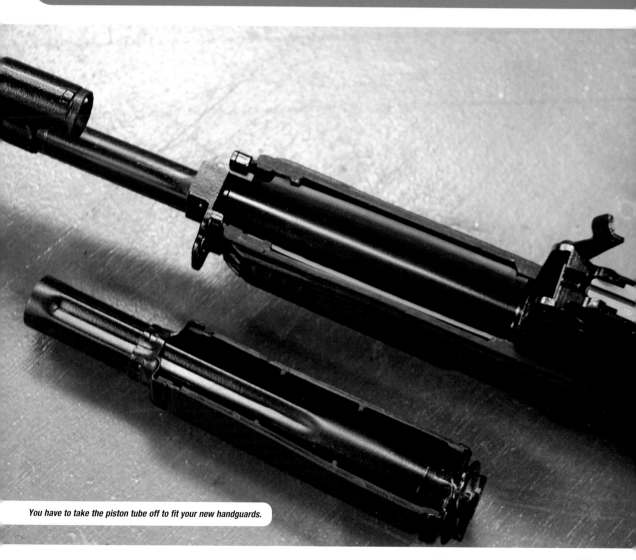

You have to take the piston tube off to fit your new handguards.

The front retainer lock needs to be pried loose before you can push the retainer forward.

You can see from these two receivers the problems handguard makers face. What fits one won't fit the other. And there are lots more varieties.

Once loose, the retainer slips forward on the barrel, freeing the handguard.

The SureFire handguard has lots of rails, and locks in tightly once fitted.

Above: You have to get your rifle to this point before you can start installing your new handguards.

Check the fit of the rear of the new handguard. If it won't go, you'll have to either send it back or modify the handguard.

Count the parts, make sure you have them all, and have Loctite handy for when you do the final assembly.

The Tech-Sight fits in the recoil spring slot in the rear trunnion. Make sure it is a tight, non-binding fit.

of the old handguard. There are some things to be aware of. First, there is no Soviet mil-spec for the size, shape or location of the opening on the front face of the receiver that your handguard fits into. It can be gaping, as in "all the space not filled by trunnion and sheet metal receiver" or it can be small, as in "Comrade, mill a narrow slot for that handguard."

The railed handguard makers are not (repeat: absolutely NOT) going to offer multiple sizes for all the various handguard openings. They have a hard enough time keeping things under control with Romanian, Chinese and Yugoslavian variants. I'm not sure the arsenals making AKs even bothered to standardize that gap for all their own rifles. So, unless your AK has the "canyon of handguard" spec opening, you will have to file, machine, grind or carve the end tab of your new one to make sure it fits the receiver opening. Also, the distance to the front handguard retainer was not a mil-spec. I'm sure the individual factories knew what they were making it to, but there certainly wasn't a Warsaw Pact-wide memo going out that said, "Comrades, the distance from the front receiver face to the center of the front handguard retainer machine cut will be XYZ millimeters, plus or minus One mm." Things just weren't that precise, or organized.

So, you may find that your retainer won't fit (in which case you have to trim some) or is too loose. You can prevent the latter by being cautious on trimming the rear to fit. Leave the rear a bit long and wide as you fit it, and if you need to shorten it, great. If you cut the rear too much, the front will be loose, and now you're really in trouble.

The next problem: your upper is not going to fit over the wood of your piston tube. Life is like that. You'll have to pry the wood off, which isn't going to

Once your railed handguard is on, tight, and you've checked function, then you can start bolting goodies to it.

When Mikhail Kalashnikov first conceived of his rifle, no one outside of science fiction could have anticipated all this bolted to it.

Right: Specialty rifles will call for heavily-modified handguards, and an involved installation. If you have something really off the beaten track, you might want to have a pro install your handguards.

Check the fit of the top half before you install the piston tube. Then install the piston tube and check fit again. This is all hand-fitted work, and you can't be too meticulous.

Once it all fits, then Loctite the screws to keep it together.

be neat and easy. The wood is meant to be there for the life of the rifle, so you'll be destroying it in order to save it. If you want to be able to switch back and forth between your railed forearm and your original, you might consider buying a new piston tube. You'll have to hand-fit your new tube (along with busting the wood off of it) but since you're going to be hand-fitting the railed handguard anyway, what's the big deal?

So far, I've found railed handguards from Krebs Custom, SureFire, and UTG. You can also bolt rail sections to Tapco Galil handguards, which is a way to get rails without the heat and cold of anodized aluminum on your hands.

I'd love to give you the essential set of instructions on installing your handguard set, but I can't. That's because the handguards, especially the railed ones, create a "perfect storm" of gunsmithing headaches. The AKs you readers have were made in separate plants over decades of time, in a severe climate of "bend to fit, paint to match" standards. Not a problem in buying or building AKs, as you're hand-fitting everything anyway. Add to that the dimensional decisions made by each individual railed handguard manufacturer. Yes, they work hard (at least some do) to get the dimensions as close as they can. But there is only so

Sighting System

The AK has the finest SMG sight system the world knew of, circa 1947. No, really. The AK is basically an SMG on steroids anyway, and the Soviets were for a long time depending on the well-known "swarming infantry" strategy, so who needed sights good for more than 50 yards? The fact that we can use them at greater distance does not negate their limits.

To improve the sights, we have four companies. Two of them, Mojo Sights and Krebs Custom, simply replace the open blade with an aperture sight. The basic Mojo sight is the AKM, with a small set-screw to fine-tune your vertical on the zero. Mojo offers a click-adjustable rear, the AKMC, where you can dial-in the rear sight height to get your Kalashnikov zeroed. Both the Mojo AKM and AKMC allow you to do some fine-tuning on windage adjustments, too. The rear aperture is in a dovetail that has a set screw adjustment. The Krebs are aperture, and you have to do zero adjustments on the front sight, as with any AK.

The rear-sight-as-aperture works, but there are limits. Your eye has to work at aiming with the aperture so far forward, but they both do improve accuracy. As for speed in-close, what I find works is to treat the AK sights like a double bead setup on a shotgun. "Both front and rear close to each other? Check. On the target? Check. Fire at will."

Installing the Mojo or Krebs is easy. Well, conceptually easy; mechanically it can be real work. Look at your rear sight. See that thing up front that looks like a pivot pin? It is. What it isn't is a captured pin. Like the Mauser 98, it is an integral part of the rear sight blade. I've seen more than one Mauser and AK horribly mangled because someone tried to drive that "pin" out of the sight.

To remove the rear sight, lock the rifle in a secure cradle or vise. Press down very hard to compress the sight spring, and pull the sight out to the rear. To install the new one, simply insert the ears on the new sight into the slot of the sight tower and push forward. You may have to whack it with a rawhide mallet to overcome the spring tension.

For greater precision, and speed as well, Tech-Sights has an aperture that rides at the back of your receiver. There, you get the precision of an aperture with the speed of a ghost ring. The

The Mojo sights can be fine-tuned to zero, and simply replace the original rear sight.

Left: You can see here the receiver lug on the handguard. Will it fit? Only checking will tell. Above: Here the gunsmith checks the fit of the handguard to the receiver gap. In this case, no problem. Below: If you want to swap back and forth, you might invest in a replacement piston tube you can bust the wood off of, and then fit it to your rifle.

much they can do, given the allowed tolerance drift of the original manufacturers.

So, instead of instructions on the method, I'll detail the process of fitting a gunsmith would go through. When you order yours, don't just ask for a "generic AK railed handguard." There isn't such a thing, and you'll get whatever they have the most of in stock. Mention the specific model you have. "A Romanian 7.62 parts

one they sent me is a prototype, and the production models will be streaming out the doors by the time this is published. Before you go to assemble the Tech-Sight aperture to your rifle, you need to make sure it fits. Take the receiver cover off, and remove the recoil spring, carrier and bolt. Now take the Tech-Sight aperture sight and see if it fits into the "T" slot of the recoil spring assembly. Those slots are not any kind of mil-spec dimension, and even if the Soviets did insist on a particular dimension it didn't matter if it wobbled, right comrade? For us it does.

The Tech-sight housing has small allen-head screws for taking up the slop in fit. If you have the screws turned in all the way and it still won't fit, you'll have to do some filing. The best way would be to file the rifle, as a loose fit of the recoil spring doesn't matter. But, it is a lot easier to file on the Tech-Sight (if you have to) so that's where I'd be turning my attentions. Don't be too eager to go filing, as I found that when trying to fit the Tech-sight to a bunch of rifles, the problem of a tight fit was often burrs or machine marks that were easy to stone or rub down, and then the sight fit. Get the assembly to be a snug, but not binding fit, as less wobble here means more potential accuracy later.

The assembly is a bit different, and you will need their dustcover. Pick up the recoil spring assembly you extracted from your rifle. You have to take it apart or buy the necessary parts to assemble a new one. Compress the spring and wriggle the end cap off the center struts. Then assemble the old spring, old front part of the strut, and the end cap, onto the Tech-Sights rear sight assembly. Stuff the bolt and carrier back into the rifle. Shove the recoil spring in, and insert the Tech-Sight just as you would when

re-installing a recoil spring. Make sure the Tech-Sight rides all the way back in the slot.

Now take the new receiver cover, and compress those two buttons you see on the sides of the Tech-Sight. Push the cover over and past those buttons, until you can snap the front down into the retaining lip on the rear sight tower. Then push the cover forward until the buttons snap up into the holes in the cover.

What of the old rear sight? Use it to rough-zero your Tech-Sight, then remove it.

Last, best and coolest is the sight from La Rue. The design-elves at LaRue have come up with a replacement rear sight that is also a red-dot sight mount, red-dot included. You have the dot from the sight, and if the battery dies you still have a rear blade. Simply remove the old sight, and install the whole LaRue assembly.

Dave Fortier has dropped targets out past 400 meters with Finnish AKs (and that wonderful Lapua ammo) and I have regularly dealt ballistic justice to 300 meter pop-ups on the National Guard base range I frequent. That we can do so is more a measure of the practice and sweat we've put in learning how to run them, than any testimonial about the inherent accuracy of the Kalashnikov. It wasn't designed to be a precision rifle. It wasn't designed to be a long-range sniping platform. However, that doesn't mean we have to settle for sights that only promise minute-of-miscreant accuracy, and sometimes actually deliver.

We're 21st century shooters and consumers. We insist on more, and as this is a capitalist, market-driven economy, we can have it.

The AK barrel has no hope of ever being free-floated. Look at all this stuff pinned to it or bearing on it.

Even with rails, you may be limited as to what you can mount, and where. This SureFire just fits.

An X200 makes a compact installation on your railed AK, but one that puts out a lot of light.

kit build, fixed stock and shark-fin handguard." Or, "A Romak 7.62 I picked up at the local big-box store" or "a Finnish Valmet in .223 bought in 1981." Don't be surprised if there aren't any handguards for that last one, or that the dealer wants to buy it.

First, check the packaging to make sure that all that is supposed to be there, is there. It really sucks to try and return a product after you've been filing on it. Or asking a manufacturer to quick send you the missing bolts you need to assemble, once you've torn the rifle apart to install the handguard. Next, strip and clean your AK, and set the old parts aside in a box or bag. This process will take a bit of time, and you don't want to lose stuff. Make sure you have the correct screwdrivers or allen wrenchs, and a bottle of Loctite. The handguard will be subject to heat and vibration, and you don't want it coming loose.

Read the instructions. I know, we're all experienced riflemen here, but you'd be surprised what a little preparation can do for your ability to assemble a seemingly simple product.

Begin by checking the fit of the lower handguard to the rifle. Does it fit the rear? Can you slide the front retainer in place and lock it down? If so, cool, you're mostly done. If not, see exactly where you have to relieve (and how much) to make the lower half slide back enough to lock in. It's too loose? Then you'll have to box it up and send it back, unless you're experienced at making loose parts fit properly.

File the tight parts to fit, checking as you go. You want to sneak up on this, as you'll get just one chance. Once it fits without force or binding, lock it in place by sliding the front retainer back and closing the lever.

Now take the upper half, and without the piston tube, see if the second part of the railed handguard ifts. It should, but if it hits or binds on the gas port block, you have to modify the handguard. Check the fit of any locking or securing screws. Most railed handguards use some kind of locking screws, since the top half isn't attached permanently to the piston tube. Some, like the SureFire, go front-to-back, others, like the Krebs, go in from the side. Once the handguard fits, remove it, install the piston tube, and re-set the handguard top in place. It will probably be a tight fit, but this is one time when you are allowed to force something in place.

Before you go and bolt it all together, pick up your carrier, slide it into the upper, and make sure the piston slides freely in and out of the piston tube. Then you can remove the screws one at a time, apply Loctite, re-install and move on to the next. Once assembled, install the bolt and carrier, recoil spring and receiver cover. Hand-cycle the action to make sure it works as-intended. Grab an empty magazine and make sure you can insert and remove it without problem.

One way to avoid a lot of this hassle is to go with a CAA handguard set. They are synthetic, and will fit many models, but if you were looking for something rigid on which to mount a red-dot scope, the CAA set might not suit your needs. But they are easier to install than aluminum ones, and will hold lights and laser with satisfaction.

SOURCES

Krebs Custom
847-487-7776
www.krebscustomAK47.com

Tech-sights
843-332-8222
www.tech-sights.com

Mojo Sights
208-255-5276
www.mojosights.com

LaRue Tactical
512-259-1585
www.laruetactical.com

SureFire
800-828-8809
www.surefire.com

CAA
754-205-9385
usa.caagearup.com

Tapco
800-554-1445
www.tapco.com

AMMUNITION FOR THE

A TALE OF TWO CARTRIDGES: THE 7.62x39mm AND 5.45x39mm.

AVTOMAT KALASHNIKOVA

TEXT AND PHOTOS BY **PETER G. KOKALIS**

Ammunition for the AK centers on two cartridges, the original 7.62x39mm round and the subsequent 5.45x39mm. Although, it should be remembered that AKs of one type or another have also been chambered for two NATO calibers—the 5.56 NATO round (as seen in the current Russian Izmash AK101 and AK102 rifles, with 415mm and 314mm barrel lengths, respectively) and the 7.62 NATO cartridge found in the Yugo-slavian M77B1 Light Machine Gun (LMG). In addition, 5.56 NATO-chambered Kalashnikov-type rifles have been produced, principally for export, by Romania (Model 97), Poland (Model 96 Beryl and Mini-Beryl), Finland (Sako M95) and the Norinco Type 97 bullpup from the People's Republic of China.

Studying and collecting military small arms ammunition is a fascinating pastime. Except for a few rare specimens, it's a lot less expensive to accumulate cartridges than the rifles for which they are chambered. As with stamp collecting, a great deal can be learned about a nation's history, culture and degree of industrial development by studying the cartridges they have manufactured. Even more important, a detailed examination of small arms cartridges is a useful tool of the technical intelligence community. During

the 1980s civil war in El Salvador, I was able to track which Com-Bloc countries were supplying the FMLN Marxist terrorists and how this changed over time by studying the headstamps of captured ammunition. For these purposes, I have provided a unique identification chart of the two principal AK cartridges at the end of the text. It's hoped that this may assist Coalition troops who read this in identifying ammunition caches, as well as stimulating budding cartridge collectors. But first let's take a close look at the history of these two cartridges and their respective wound-ballistics potential.

Caliber 7.62x39mm cartridge cases are principally of three types, left to right: brass, copper-washed steel and lacquered steel in varying shades of gray, OD or brown lacquer.

A series of draws made by dies are used to form a cartridge case. Left: brass pellet after the first draw; center: two intermediate-stage draws of copper-washed steel Cuban cases found in the ballast bag of a Cuban freighter in an Italian harbor; right: finished 7.62x39mm ball cartridge.

M43 CARTRIDGE

Attributed to designers Nikolai M. Elizarov and Boris V. Semin, Soviet historians contend that work on the M43 (Model 1943) 7.62x39mm cartridge began in 1939, was temporarily suspended because of the Great Patriotic War and then recommenced and finalized in 1943. Others have stated that it was derived from the German 7.92x33mm Kurz Patrone (short cartridge) developed for the world's first assault rifle produced in significant quantities, the World War II MP43/44 (StG44/45). This latter scenario is highly unlikely, as the Soviets would have required specimens of 7.92x33mm Kurz ammunition at least a year or two prior to their adoption of the 7.62x39mm round in 1943, well before the MP43 was fielded on the Osten front (first reported use was December 1942).

Whatever the case, the Soviet M43 cartridge is a true intermediate assault-rifle round. The first prototypes featured cases that were 40.29mm in length (thus: 7.62x41mm). The case was trimmed to 38.6mm, as the original projectile proved unsatisfactory; a new bullet was adopted that required a shorter case.

The following countries have manufactured ammunition in this caliber: Austria, Belgium,

Color codes on a projectile's tip are used to identify the type of ammunition. Left to right, caliber 7.62x39mm East German gallery round with roundnose plastic bullet, Egyptian tracer and armor-piercing incendiary rounds.

Brazil, Bulgaria, Cuba, Czechoslovakia, East Germany, Egypt, Finland, France, Hungary, Iraq, Israel, Netherlands, North Korea, Norway, Peru, Poland, Portugal, People's Republic of China, Romania, South Africa, South Korea, Sweden, Syria, United States, U.S.S.R., West Germany and Yugoslavia. In addition to Full Metal Jacket (FMJ) ball ammunition, it has been produced with hollowpoint, softpoint, tracer, API (armor-piercing incendiary) and IT (incendiary tracer) projectiles.

Special-purpose loads have included heavy subsonic ball (for use with sound suppressors), practice blanks, short-range loads and drill rounds. Ball ammunition will be encountered in two configurations. Most prevalent is a 123-grain boat-tail bullet, which usually consists of a copper-washed steel jacket, lead and antimony sleeve and a mild steel core (Soviet Type PS). Yugoslavia's M67 ball ammunition, as well as that of several other countries, uses a flat-based bullet of approximately the same weight with a copper-alloy jacket and lead core. Muzzle velocity of both types is between 2,330 and 2,400 fps.

In its boattail configuration, the 7.62x39mm FMJ bullet travels point-forward about 10 inches in soft tissue before significant yaw occurs. At that distance the bullet will yaw to less than 90 degrees, then come back down to a point-forward position and finally yaw 180 degrees—ending its travel in a base-forward position. Bi-lobed yaw cycles of this type are commonly observed with pointed, nondeforming bullets. Total penetration in living tissue is almost 29 inches. Abdominal shots usually exhibit no greater tissue disruption than that produced by a .38 Special bullet fired from a handgun since, after 10 inches of travel without yawing, the bullet has generally passed through the abdominal cavity. However, of course, this round is capable of inflicting such damage at far greater ranges than a handgun would. When I was working at the Wound Ballistics Laboratory at the Letterman Army Institute of Research in San Francisco, we tested the lead-cored, flat-base Yugoslav bullet and found it to be considerably more effective. It commences its yaw cycle after only three to four inches of penetration. Once again, the yaw cycle is generally bi-lobed. The bullet reaches its maximum penetration of 23 to 26 inches traveling base-forward, somewhat flattened and retaining almost all of its original weight (two or three small fragments are shed in the area of maximum cavitation).

Although the flat-based 7.62x39mm bullet is shorter (.930 inch) than the more common boattail projectile (1.040 inch), it will be expected to cause more damage to the abdomen, liver, spleen or pancreas because the bullet passes through these organs at a large yaw angle. If we have neither mushrooming nor fragmentation, yawing is all that remains to maximize tissue disruption

The 7.62x39mm cartridge has been utilized in not only assault rifles but also squad automatics like the RPD and RPK (seen here with 75-round drum) and even Designated Marksman Rifles (DMR) like the Iraqi Tabuk.

and enhance the bullet's performance—provided that we do not sacrifice penetration.

THE 5.45X39MM CARTRIDGE

Development of the 5.45x39mm cartridge was quite obviously in direct response to the 5.56x45mm NATO M193 56-grain ball round, deployed with arguable success in Vietnam. Research on the concept began in the late 1960s. Engineer Viktor Sabelnikov headed the project.

The rimless 5.45x39mm bottlenecked steel case is actually 39.6mm in length. The 53-grain boattail bullet has a gilding-metal-clad steel jacket. The unhardened flat-tip steel core is covered by a

Kalashnikovs chambered for the 7.62x39mm cartridge were produced by a number of nations. Top to bottom: Finnish Valmet M62, an AK-47-type with a mill-finished forged receiver; Hungarian AMD-65, an AKM-type with a stamped-sheetmetal receiver and 20-round magazine peculiar to this model; and Yugoslavian M92, a so-called Krinkov-type.

Finland produced a wide variety of caliber 7.62x39mm plastic training blanks in somewhat startling colors with rather strange "duckbill" and three-sided chisel-point projectile heads for use with the Valmet Kalashnikov-type rifles in service with its armed forces.

Caliber 7.62x39mm dummy training rounds, used to cycle the rifle manually, appear in a wide variety of case configurations and construction. The round in the center, which is from the People's Republic of China, has both a black plastic bullet and primer.

lead sleeve that does not fill the entire interior of the jacket, leaving a hollow cavity inside the nose—the focal point of the imbroglio over wounding potential.

Large-caliber steel cores, such as the hardened penetrator of the U.S. .50-caliber AP round, can be screw-turned to a pointed tip without too much trouble. It would be difficult to screw-turn, or even swage, a pointed tip on the 5.45x39mm bullet's small steel core. I personally believe it was simply more cost-effective to fabricate a flat-tipped core and leave an air pocket under the jacket's tip as long as it did not affect the projectile's aerodynamic qualities. The fact that it might enhance the bullet's wounding potential was, in this instance, merely coincidental. (Some reliable Russian sources plainly state the design of the 7N6 projectile was in part to enhance terminal performance.)

There is nothing new about this type of construction. During World War I, the British .303-inch Mark VII bullet contained an aluminum (and sometimes fiber, wood, pottery or compressed paper) filler in front of its lead and antimony core, directly under the jacket's tip. This was principally an attempt to reduce the bullet's weight.

With one peculiar exception, the 5.45x39mm bullet exhibits no more, or less, than the usual performance characteristics expected from a nondeforming Full Metal Jacket (FMJ) military bullet. There is a rather typical bi-lobe yaw cycle in soft tissue, with the bullet ending its travel base-forward. Yaw commences after only about three inches of penetration in living tissue. This will increase the tissue disruption, even in many extremity hits on the arms or legs.

In all tests performed on this cartridge by Dr. Martin L. Fackler

Although adopted by the Soviet army in 1974, the 5.45x39mm cartridge never proved as popular as the older 7.62x39mm. Here are a few Kalashnikovs chambered for the newer round, top to bottom: Polish Tantal AK74 (known in Poland as the wzor-88), Russian AK105 selective-fire version three-shot-burst mode and Bulgarian "Krinkov" (a complete misnomer) with 8.5-inch barrel.

Examining the base of a cartridge case usually provides the most valuable source of information concerning its origin. Caliber 7.62x39mm cartridges from left to right: Cuban CWS case with "13" code, East German LSC with "04" code, Egyptian BSC with "27" code in Arabic script and Dutch BSC with "NWM" for Nederlandsche Wapen-En Munitiefabriek.

Caliber 7.62x39mm blank cartridges: the two at the far right are training-type, which will function in a weapon equipped with a BFA (Blank Firing Attachment); the other rounds were intended for launching rifle grenades.

at the Wound Ballistics Laboratory, the angle of this bullet's long axis after it came to rest in the tissue simulant showed a change in direction of between 80 and 90 degrees. Curvature of a boattail FMJ bullet's path is not uncommon, but always sporadic and generally no more than 45 degrees. X-rays taken at the Wound Ballistics Lab of recovered 5.45x39mm bullets showed that the lead sleeve flowed asymmetrically forward into the jacket tip after rapid deceleration upon striking tissue, to unbalance the projectile and possibly initiate its right-angle turn. Curious, but the results are less than awesome. When the AK74 rifle and its cartridge first surfaced in Afghanistan, rumors were widely circulated that its muzzle velocity exceeded 4,000 fps, and that it produced massive tissue damage. Obviously, this was not true. The performance approximates that of the M193 round, albeit for somewhat different reasons.

The ammunition used in my tests and

evaluations of rifles chambered for the 5.45x39mm cartridge was imported by Wolf Performance Ammunition and manufactured at Tula Cartridge Works in Russia. Headstamped "5.45X39 WOLF," the lacquered steel case has a red case mouth sealant and primer annulus. The flattened ball, single-base nitrocellulose propellant has a charge weight of 20½ grains, nominal. Although the packaging stated the projectile to be 60 grains, it was in fact 59 grains, nominal.

It is claimed that this bullet provides the same wound-ballistic characteristics as the standard Russian 7N6 military round, but I have not confirmed this. Chronographing this ammunition through a Polish Tantal rifle produced the following results. All chronograph tests were conducted with a PACT MKIV timer with chronograph and cyclic rate counter. Velocities were measured

Development of the 5.45x39mm cartridge was quite obviously in direct response to the U.S. 5.56x45mm NATO M193 round deployed in Vietnam. Left: East Germany gallery round with white plastic projectile; right: East German caliber 5.45x39mm ball ammunition.

at a distance of 10 feet from the muzzle. The ambient temperature at the time of the tests was 79 degrees Farenheit.

The average velocity from a 16¼-inch barrel was about 3,020 fps. The extreme spread of velocities varied from 57 to 74 fps. The standard variation ranged from 18 to 28 fps, while the MAD (Mean Absolute Deviation) as a percent of the average velocity was about .55 percent; that is excellent and indicates almost match-grade ammunition.

Accuracy has long been an area of criticism with the Kalashnikov series. Very rarely will any AK shoot better than three or four MOA. Ammunition is usually part of the problem, as true match-grade ball ammo is rarely available. In addition, the AK's exceptional reliability is partially a result of manufacturing tolerances designed to maximize reliability under adverse conditions. This, without doubt, affects the rifle's accuracy potential.

However, the question remains: how much accuracy is necessary, or even desired, for a battlefield infantry rifle? In most instances the Kalashnikov is "good enough for government work" with the usual high level of reliability and accuracy intended for the battlefield, not bullseye paper targets.

7.62x39mm AND 5.45x39mm
CARTRIDGE IDENTIFICATION GUIDE

THE MOST IMPORTANT INFORMATION used to determine the origin of a cartridge is found at the base of the cartridge case. At that location will be found what is called the headstamp, which is placed there by what is called a bunter during the series of draws made by dies that form the cartridge case through several distinct stages. The information usually, but not always, found on the headstamp indicates the arsenal of manufacture, the year of manufacture (usually just the last two digits) and the caliber. This information is most often embossed into the head of the case, but sometimes, such as on Russian caliber 7.62x54R cases, it will be found as raised letters and numerals.

There are other characteristics that can help us determine the origin of a cartridge. The nature of the case itself is useful, as it can be made of brass, copper-washed steel, brass-washed steel or lacquered steel. The color and type of the primer annulus (the sealer around the primer) and the case mouth or projectile sealant, if present, can also indicate the origin. For example, the primer annulus and case mouth sealant from the arsenal in Yugoslavia are a distinctive red-orange used by no other manufacturer. The color tip of a bullet can indicate the type of projectile—such as ball, tracer, armor-piercing incendiary or incendiary tracer—and sometimes also the origin.

Below is a detailed list of this data, as found on hundreds of cartridges in the calibers 7.62x39mm and 5.45x39mm.

The abbreviations used in the list are: CWS = copper-washed steel case, BrWS = brass-washed steel case, BRS = brass case, LSC = lacquered steel case, cm = case mouth, OD = olive drab, ann = primer annulus, seal = projectile sealant, proj = projectile, RN = roundnose, HP = hollowpoint, SP = softpoint, API = armor-piercing incendiary and IT = incendiary tracer.

7.62X39MM CARTRIDGES

COUNTRY OF ORIGIN	FACTORY CODE - HEADSTAMP	OTHER FEATURES	Type
Austria	HP *7,62x39	green, red or purple; ann; BRS or OD LSC	ball
Belgium	FN with 70, 76, or 77	purple or no ann; BRS	ball
Brazil	CBC or MRP with 7.62x39 and sometimes a date	purple ann; BRS	ball
Bulgaria	10 with dates from 57 to 94	red or no ann; LSC; green tip for tracer	various
Cuba	13 with dates from 81 to 87	red ann and seal; CWS	ball
Czechoslovakia	ZV, bxn or aym from 54 to 87	black primer; gray LSC fluted-case dummies; green tip for tracer	various
East Germany	04 or 05 dates from 62 to 88	no ann, purple or red ann OD LSC; green tip for tracer	various
Egypt	mostly 27, but also 03 39; dates from 59 to 90	red or purple ann; BRS black/red tip for API, green tip for tracer	various
Finland	mostly VPT, but also PT, LAPUA, SO, SAKO or 539	no ann; BRS; numerous plastic training rounds; white tip for tracer	various
Hungary	21 or 23; dates from 60 to 88	red or no ann; gray LSC black/red tip for API, green tip for tracer	various
Iraq	(Arabic script) (69)	no ann; BRS	ball
Israel	IMI 7.62x39	no ann; BRS	ball or SP
Netherlands	NWM 7.62x38 59 date	black or red ann, BRS	ball

COUNTRY OF ORIGIN	FACTORY CODE - HEADSTAMP	OTHER FEATURES	TYPE
North Korea	93 or Korean script dates from 74 to 85	no ann; CWS; green tip for tracer	various
Norway	no markings	colored plastic bodies w/aluminum projectiles	blank
Peru	F A M E 7.62x39	green ann; BRS	ball
Poland	21 or 343 with inverted dates from 57 to 82	no or red ann; OD LSC	ball
Portugal	7.62x39 FNM with 2-digit date and -1 or -2	green ann; BRS	ball
People's Republic of China	numerous arsenals: 31, 51, 61, 71, 81, 101, 111, 121, 131, 141, 201, 301, 311, 321, 341, 351, 391, 501, 601, 651, 661, 671, 811,921, 946, 948, 964, 6201, 6202, 6203, 9121, 9141 and 7.62X39 CNIC	green or red ann; red proj seal; CWS or green LSC; black tip for API; green tip for tracer; many dummy training rounds with black plastic bullets	various
Romania	R P R 22, 22, 323, 32, 324, 325 with 2-digit year date, or no code with date only	red proj seal and red or green ann, gray LSC with green tip for tracer	various
South Africa	12 or 13 with 87 or 88 date	red or no ann; BRS	ball
South Korea	PMC 7.62X39MM	red or no ann; BRS	ball
Sweden	NORMA 7.62X39	no ann; BRS	ball
Syria	39x7.62 or 7.62x39 *64 *(64 to 80)	red or purple proj seal/ann; BRS	ball
United States	none, L C 7 1, MIDWAY 7.62X39, F C 7.62 x 39, R - P 7.62 X 39mm 101, bxn 53 1 (reworked 7.62x45mm - T.C.C.I.), W C C 7.62 X 39, WINCHESTER 7.62 x 39	red ann; BRS	ball
USSR	numerous arsenals: 3, 17, 60, 270, 539, 711, dates from 51 to 93 [sometimes in Cyrillic]	red proj seal and ann; mostly CWS, some green LSC; black/red tip for API, green tip for tracer	various
West Germany	none or 01 71	green ann; BRS	ball
Yugoslavia	nny (Cyrillic with 4-digit date), IK with 2-digit date, NK (Cyrillic wwith 4-digit date)	red-orange ann, occasionally violet ann; green tip for tracer; BRS or gray LSC	various

5.45x39mm CARTRIDGES

Bulgaria	10 with 2-digit dates in the 80s	red proj seal and ann; LSC	ball
East Germany	05 with 2-digit dates in the 80s	red proj seal and ann; LSC; green tip for tracer, white plastic bullet for gallery round	various
West Germany	R W S 215	no ann; LSC	JHP
Romania	323 with 2-digit dates in the 80s	red proj seal and ann; LSC	ball
U.S.S.R.	numerous arsenals: 3, 17, 60, 270 and 539 with 2-digit dates from 76 to mid 90s	red proj seal and ann; LSC; green tip for tracer and white plastic bullet for gallery round	various

There are undoubtedly omissions and anomalies with any list of this type, which must be continuously revised and updated. Nevertheless, most 7.62x39mm and 5.45x39mm cartridges can be identified by matching their salient characteristics with the rounds on this chart.

FEEDING YOUR
KALASHNIKOV

IDENTIFYING AND COLLECTING AK-47 MAGS.
BY **EDWARD T. MCLEAN**

The AK's rugged, thick-lipped magazine will probably outlast your rifle, one of the major selling points of this particular design.

When this article was first visualized several years back, it was planned to be all encompassing, on all magazines and for all AK variants. It didn't take long to realize that such a scope was impractical. This effort is thus limited to 7.62x39mm magazines with a capacity of 30 rounds or less and that don't need to be modified to work in a standard AK. Even with this seemingly narrow scope, the project proved dauntingly large and continued to grow every few months as new variations showed up.

RUSSIA

When the Soviet Union started production of the AK-47 in late 1948 at the Izhevsk Machine Plant, also known as Izhmash, the AK-47 came with a 30-round magazine generally referred to as the Russian Slab-Side, the name coming from the distinctive smooth sides stamped into its body. This blued-finish magazine is generally covered in inspector stamps, but the Izhmash factory mark (feathered arrow in triangle) will be found stamped low on its back. Made from thick 1mm steel, it is both durable and heavy. It was only produced by Izhmash for a few years before the design was replaced.

About the time that the Type III AK-47 was adopted in 1954, a new, lighter 30-round steel magazine was introduced. Made from thinner steel (.75mm versus 1mm), it had ribs stamped into the body for added strength. The body, as with the earlier Slab-Side version, was formed from two stamped-metal halves that were spot-welded together along the front and along the rear flanges (referred to as the magazine spine). Each side has three outward-facing horizontal ribs, one inward-facing horizontal rib and five outward-facing horizontal ribs along the bottom of the magazine. Three of these horizontal ribs are noticeably short and basically just wrap around the bottom rear of the magazine. The first ribbed magazines had the inward-facing rib at the rear of the magazine's body going straight up and under the plates that reinforce each feed lip. This type of magazine was also produced by many other countries and will be referred to here as the First European Ribbed Type.

The earliest Soviet ribbed magazine, the Izhmash Back-Stamped Ribbed Magazine, has the Izhmash factory mark on the bottom back of the magazine like the Russian Slab-Side. At first they were blued, but this was eventually changed to a baked-on black enamel finish. Izhmash reportedly switched to an enamel finish on its AKs shortly before production of the AKM rifle began in 1959. The followers on these early magazines will have a large, pill-shaped bulge with a hole through its front left side. This bulge does not extend to the rear of the follower.

Eventually, the Izhmash factory mark was moved to the spine, and this version is generally referred to as the Early Izhmash Spine-Stamped Magazine. This magazine eventually received a new follower with a longer, thinner bulge that extends to the rear of the follower. The hole through the front left side of the follower's bulge was also eliminated.

At some point the dies used by Izhmash to stamp magazine bodies were redesigned. The inward-facing ribs, at the back of the magazine, now stop short of the feed-lip reinforcement plates

and turn at a 90-degree angle toward the rear. These ribs will resemble an upside-down "L" at the top. As would be expected, these will be found with the Izhmash mark stamped on the spine and a baked-on black enamel finish. Collectors generally refer to them as Late Izhmash Spine-Stamped Magazines. This type was also made by many other countries, and it will be referred to here as the Second European Ribbed Type.

In 1960, the Soviet's Tula arsenal started producing the AKM. All Tula rifles, and steel magazines, are finished with a baked-on black enamel finish. Tula magazines are of the Second European Ribbed Type and will usually have a fair number of inspector stamps on both the spine and lower sides. Tula always stamped its factory mark, a five-pointed star, on the spine. Tula Steel Magazines are relatively rare, as they were only made for a few years before production was switched to a new AG4 plastic type.

The last steel magazine produced by the Soviets is referred to by collectors as the Izhmash Side-Stamped. It is basically a Late Izhmash Spine-Stamped magazine with one very noticeable difference. On the magazine's left side, the middle outward-facing vertical rib stops well before the other two, leaving a blank area at the bottom of the magazine where the Izhmash factory mark is prominently stamped. These have a black enamel finish and, as the name implies, were only made by Izhmash.

In the mid-to-late 1950s, the Soviets also produced an aluminum

30-round AK magazine generally referred to as the Aluminum Waffle by collectors because of its very distinctive ribbed pattern. These magazines are made entirely of aluminum, except for its spring, and has a black enamel finish. They are found with multiple inspector stamps on both the spine and lower sides. They were made by Izhmash, and most will show its factory mark on their spine. They were probably discontinued in favor of the steel magazine's greater strength. Soldiers have been known to use their magazines as hammers and even bottle openers.

During the early 1960s, the Soviets introduced a new 30-round AK magazine made from a glass-fiber-reinforced plastic called AG4. This reddish-orange magazine was molded in two halves that were then joined with an epoxy adhesive, steel front and rear lugs being molded into the body. The follower, keeper/takedown plate and floorplate also remained steel. These Russian AG4 Plastic Magazines were made by both Tula and Izhmash, the respective arsenal's mark being molded into the bottom right side of the magazine, while the mold number is on the bottom left side. Inspector marks were stamped onto the body with permanent ink. It is interesting to note that they never fully replaced the steel magazine in Russian service. Reportedly, this was due in no small part to soldiers' fears that if they were injured, shards of a plastic magazine would not show up in an X-ray.

Between the two manufacturers, a large number of variations of the Russian AG4 plastic magazine exist. Very early magazines have a mold line that gives the impression of a long top, but the molds were quickly redesigned to move the mold line higher up on the body. They will also be found with, and without, a noticeable ridge running down their back, and at least four types of floorplates are known to exist. Izhmash also had at least two sizes of its factory mark molded into the body.

During the 1980s, the Soviets experimented with a plum-colored polymer 30-round AK-47 magazine, at a time when they were manufacturing a similar magazine for use in their 5.45x39 AK74 rifles. Like the AK74 magazine, steel lugs were molded into the body and it uses a steel floorplate. Criss-crossing ribs, however, were molded into the body for added strength and possibly quick identification of its caliber. These Russian Plum Waffle Magazines unfortunately lack any markings to indicate the arsenal that made them. Only a handful of these have made their way into the U.S., and it is probably the most sought-after AK magazine.

At the present time, the Russian Izhmash factory is making a 7.62x39mm black polymer 30-round magazine for export sales with its AK103/AK104 rifles. None of these has ever been directly imported into the U.S., but some have reportedly made their way here through a third country. The magazine made for Izhmash's Siaga version of the AK is often modified to work in a regular AK and then incorrectly represented as one of these.

BULGARIA

In 1958, the Bulgarians began production of the AK-47 at their Factory 10 under Russian license. The earliest Bulgarian steel magazines were of the First European Ribbed Type and are seen stamped with

either a "10" or an "E" in a double circle on the spine. The "E" in a double circle may have come about in 1964 when Factory 10 was temporarily renamed United Industrial Plant "Friederich Engels," but it more likely represents a different factory. All of these early magazines appear to have a blued finish and the large pill-shaped bulge, with hole, on their followers. The follower's bulge is similar to the earliest Russian ribbed mags, but not rounded as much.

The next Bulgarian steel magazine is of the Second European Ribbed Type. These will be found with both the earlier follower and a new follower featuring an elongated bulge without hole. All the marked ones examined carried the stamped "E" in a double circle on the spine. Most appear to have a phosphate finish.

The third Bulgarian steel pattern is a truly unique type. The inward-facing rib on the rear top left side of the magazine expands backward in a slanted concave shape to the feed-lip reinforcement plate. On the right side it expands backward in a slanted convex shape. Early magazines have a phosphate finish, while the later/majority have a black enamel finish. Most of these Late Bulgarian Steel Magazines are unmarked, but a few have shown up stamped with either an "E" in a double circle or "25" in a double circle on the rear spine. The "25" in a double circle represents Optico Electron Inc., a well-known Bulgarian manufacturer of polymer AK74 magazines. (Author's note: For this article, reference will only be made to the number of outward-facing ribs on a steel magazine. The inward-facing rib at the rear will be con-

European Ribbed Types (from right): First European Ribbed Type, Second European Ribbed Type, Late Bulgarian.

sidered a given and covered by its type description.)

Around the year 2000, a series of experimental 30-round polymer waffle magazines were imported by Magua Industries from Bulgaria. Imported in only small quantities, they were advertised colored arctic white, blue, clear, gray, hunter green, olive green, plum and even yellow. However, only the arctic white, clear, hunter green and olive magazines appear to have made it here in any quantity. They carry the factory mark of a "10" in a double circle, which is molded into their left side. These magazines are strengthened by thin sheets of steel, as well as steel front and rear lugs, embedded within the polymer body. The follower and keeper/takedown plate are made of polymer, but the floorplate remained a steel stamping. The clear polymer magazines, for obvious reasons, had the steel sheets left out of the body and have suffered badly from cracking at the lips due to this fact and the type of polymer used.

A few years later large quantities of these 30-round polymer waffle magazines, now black in color, started to be imported into the U.S. Interestingly, they will sometimes be found with, and without, a mold number on the right side. These magazines were designed for military sales and have shown up in Iraq in large quantities with the new Bulgarian AKs supplied to the post-Saddam army.

The 1994 ban of so-called "assault rifles" led to more politically correct thumbhole-stocked AKs without bayonet lugs. The Bulgarians responded with the SA93 and SLR95 sporting rifles and exported them here with newly developed five- and 10-round shortened versions of the black Bulgarian Waffle. The bodies of these magazines are the same regardless of capacity, and capacity was simply increased by shortening the follower and keeper. No factory markings will be found molded into these magazines, but the follower is marked with a "5" or "10" in silver paint to indicate its capacity.

KVAR Corp. has recently had the Bulgarian arsenal produce waffle magazines for them in special colors to match the U.S.-made polymer stocks KVAR sells. Olive drab-colored magazines have been made in five-, 10-, 30- and 40-round capacities. Plum magazines have been made in 30- and 40-round capacities.

In early 2007, another type of polymer 30-round magazine was imported that is usually referred to as the Bulgarian Bullet Magazine. The name comes from the image of seven cartridges molded into each side. They also have "Cal. 7.62x39" molded into the bottom left side, as well as three small stars molded into the bottom right side. The manufacturer, ISD Bulgaria Ltd., placed no arsenal marking on these to indicate that it made them. The polymer body is reinforced with thin sheets of steel, and the floorplate remains a steel stamping. The follower and keeper are made from polymer, but, more important, so are the front and rear lugs. Unfortunately, the rocking motion used to insert a magazine into an AK will eventually wear out plastic lugs, and one should expect only a fraction of a military steel magazine's lifespan from them.

A common complaint, particularly from first-time users, regards the Bulgarian Bullet magazine's self-cleaning ability. As the follower rises up, it forces the feed lips slightly farther apart and supposedly pushes crud up and out. The increased width of such an empty magazine sometimes prevents its insertion into an AK, particularly those with U.S.-made receivers. No problems were experienced inserting empty magazines into my factory-built AKs. Loading at least three rounds in a magazine allows insertion in any AK.

The bullet images molded into the body were never much of a hit with the shooting community. They were often considered tacky. In late 2007, the Bulgarian factory redesigned the molds to remove the bullet images and replaced the three stars on the bottom right side with a symbol believed to represent the factory. The "CAL. 7.62X39" marking on the bottom left side was also made a little more prominent. Otherwise they remained unchanged, and this new version is generally referred to as the Bulgarian Slab-Side. In July 2008, a clear polymer version of this mag was introduced to the U.S. market. The Bulgarian Clear Slab-Side does not have steel reinforcements in its body.

In mid-2008, the unique Late Bulgarian Steel Magazines started showing up in the U.S. with the same black polymer follower and keeper used in the Bulgarian Bullet and Slab-Side. It would appear that ISD Bulgaria is manufacturing these new hybrid magazines in order to keep the price competitive with military surplus. They are finished with black enamel, show excellent workmanship and work very well.

EAST GERMANY
East Germany received a license from the Soviet Union in 1957 to produce the AK-47, but production didn't start until 1959. East German 30-round steel magazines are all of the First European Ribbed Type and are generally known for their excellent blued finishes. Their follower is of a unique pattern, having a bulge that is flattened at its rear, but rounded at the front. Early East German Blued magazines will almost always be found with two to six large, thin, block-style letters stamped on their spine. There is no apparent pattern to the letters stamped on the spines, and these are believed to be just inspector stamps. A single small number in an oval, such as "15," "16" and "29," is also sometimes found stamped on the spine.

Much rarer, and largely unknown, is the Late East German 30-round magazine. The body and follower remain identical to those of an early East German magazine, but it has a black phosphate finish. The thing that really makes it stand out is its unique floorplate. The normal oval-shaped stamping at the front of the floorplate instead has its rear edge flattened into a slanting straight line. The few of these examined were unmarked.

EGYPT
Egypt received a license to produce the AKM in 1971 and began production shortly afterward, initially using imported Russian parts. Egyptian 30-round magazines, surprisingly, are of the First European Ribbed Type. Early commercial examples imported to the U.S. were stamped "Made in Egypt" on their top left side. These have a glossy black enamel finish applied to the body and floorplate that is often atrocious, showing obvious dripping. The follower, however, has a blued finish. What really makes them stand out from other First European Ribbed Types is their welding patterns. The rear catch has unusual tear-drop-shaped spot welds, while the front lug, and front edge of the magazine's body, have round spot welds. The welding along the spine is neither round nor oval, and while sometimes indistinct, it is best described as a blob.

Later both 30- and five-round Egyptian magazines were imported with a matte black enamel finish on their bodies and with blued followers and floorplates. The five-round magazine was produced simply by cutting down a 30-round magazine. The follower pattern was slightly different on these magazines, and the front lug was enlarged. The welding pattern, however, remained nearly identical. No factory markings have ever been identified on an Egyptian magazine.

FINLAND
Large-scale production of Finland's version of the AK, the M62, began at both the Valmet and Sako factories in 1965. The Finnish-produced 30-round steel magazine is of the First European Ribbed Type and has a blued finish. While at first glance it may look similar to any number of magazines, it has several unique features that make it easy to pick out. First is a folding rectangular steel ring welded to the floorplate. This ring's purpose has been variously described as a means of securing the magazine to the soldier's web gear or for attaching a lanyard ring, but a Finnish veteran informed me that it is simply to give a soldier something to grab on to when removing it from a magazine pouch. Second, it has both a 10-round and 30-round witness hole in the back. All other European 30-round ribbed magazines have just a 30-round witness hole. An examination of the right side of the rear lug will most often show a "T" stamping, which reportedly comes from the Finnish word Taisteluväline, or "war material." Much less common are commercial magazines marked with an "S" instead, believed to represent either "Sako" or "Sporter."

A unique 15-round steel magazine was developed for export sales with their semi-

Floorplates (from left): Russian Slab-Side, late East German, Finnish M62 Steel and late Hungarian.

auto 7.62x39 Valmet M76 rifle. The magazine's body is stamped with just three horizontal ribs on each side. The folding rectangular ring was not welded to the floorplate, which left the rear of the floorplate noticeably flat. All other European ribbed magazine floorplates have a round-shaped stamping there.

During the early 1990s, the Finnish began developing a 30-round polymer AK magazine for their military. This bears a strong resemblance to the Bulgarian Waffle with its crisscrossing horizontal and vertical ribs. Likewise, steel front and rear lugs are molded into the body along with thin sheets of metal to strengthen the feed lips. Unlike the Bulgarian Waffle, the Finnish Waffle design uses a polymer floorplate.

Finnish Trial Waffle Magazines are dark green in color. Shortly after trial production began, a polymer loop was molded into the bottom front of the magazine and the floorplate was strengthened. When it was finally adopted, the color was changed to black and a date code was molded into one side. The few Finnish Black Waffle Magazines examined were made during the 1994 to 1997 time period. A few of these black magazines, made for commercial sale in Europe, were laser-engraved "SAKO" on the bottom right side.

HUNGARY

Hungary started manufacturing a version of the AK-47 in 1959. All Hungarian 30-round magazines are of the First European Ribbed Type. Early magazines have a blued finish and will often be found with an "02" and a smiley-faced quarter-moon stamping on the spine. They also have a very distinctive bulge on the follower that is flattened at both ends. These early follower bulges have a noticeable large hole in the front left side. At some point the finish on the magazine's components was changed to black enamel.

Few other changes will be noted in the Hungarian 30-round magazine during its long production span. The follower was eventually changed to a more traditionally oval-shaped bulge. This was followed by a small "M" in circle inspector stamp on the spine and a new floorplate with a thinner, oval-shaped stamping at its front. Large quantities of the late magazines will also be found with keepers

having only a gray phosphate finish and even with no finish.

Only a few of the late Hungarian AK magazines present a challenge to identify. These were generally made for commercial sale in the U.S. and are unmarked. An easy way to identify one, as well as any Hungarian magazine, is to disassemble it and look at its keeper. Hungarian keepers are unique among the European, and Egyptian, steel magazines in that they lack a spring guide protruding from them.

In 1965, the Hungarians adopted a compact version of the AK called the AMD-65. It was designed for specialized troops and so that a soldier could easily exit an armored vehicle carrying it. A shorter 20-round AK magazine was developed for its use. This magazine has just three vertical ribs on each side. All of these examined were finished in a black enamel finish. Changes in markings, follower shape, keeper finish and floorplate stamping followed the 30-round magazine.

The Hungarian FEG plant also produced a superb five-round magazine, with a dedicated body die, for its post-ban SA 85M rifle. This magazine clearly shows superior welding and a near flawless flat-black baked-on enamel finish. Its body features only three vertical ribs on each side. The inward-facing rib at the rear, as on all Hungarian magazines, is of the First European Ribbed Type. The follower and floorplate are the same as used on late Hungarian 30-round magazines. The keeper, with its button showing through the floorplate, has just a gray phosphate finish.

POLAND

Poland received its license to build the AK-47 in 1956 and probably started production shortly afterward. The earliest Polish 30-round magazine is of the First European Ribbed Type and bears a strong resemblance to both the earliest Russian and Bulgarian Ribbed magazines. The follower's bulge, however, more closely resembles that of the earliest Bulgarian magazine.

Unfortunately, no factory mark was placed on these Early Polish Magazines, and inspector stamps vary more than other manufacturers. Large, round inspector stamps, with numbers and letters inside, are often found stamped on the spine of the very earliest magazines. "K1" over "S/59," "PW" over "3," "K1" over "1/055" and even large, simple numbers such as a "2" or "4" stamped within these circles have been observed. A letter, a number or a combination (such as "S2" or "S7") will also often be found stamped on the spine or lower sides. Later examples are commonly seen with an "11" or "12" in a triangle stamped on the spine. Followers often show inspector stamps on their sides, something not found on either Russian or Bulgarian magazines. Polish magazines also generally show very small weld

marks (or none) on the front lug, while the Russian and Bulgarian magazines have large, obvious weld marks on the front lug.

Late Polish Magazines are of the Second European Ribbed Type and have a black phosphate finish. They feature a new follower with an elongated bulge without a hole. A few of the earliest magazines of this type will be found with an "11" or "12" in a triangle stamped on the spine like some of the Early Polish Magazines.

The vast majority of these Late Polish Magazines are unmarked and bear a strong resemblance to those from Romania. Polish magazines, however, will usually have less evident weld marks, show generally more care in construction and have a follower that differs slightly. The front of the oval bulge on the follower, that cuts inward, is shorter, slants less and is generally less noticeable than those on a Romanian magazine. The cutout on the floorplate's rear for clearance of the magazine's spine is also noticeably smaller on a Polish magazine.

Poland also manufactured a 30-round black polymer magazine, apparently during the late 1990s. The body, follower and takedown plate were made from polymer, while the floorplate remained a steel stamping. The front and rear lugs are steel embedded within the polymer body. The figures "7.62x39" were molded into the mag's body on the upper left side. All the magazines observed had a mold number of "1" or "2" on the lower left side. Unfortunately, cracked feed lips have been a serious problem with these Polish Polymer Magazines.

ROMANIA

Romania appears to have started manufacturing AKs around 1963 with its MD63 variant. All Romanian AK magazines, because of the

Factory Markings (from bottom): Soviet Izhmash, Soviet Tula, Chinese Factory 626.

late start in manufacturing, are of the Second European Ribbed Type. Some of the earliest 30-round blued magazines will be found with the Cugir factory mark of an arrowhead and shaft within a triangle on their spine that is often confused with Izhmash's complete feathered arrow in a triangle. However, most of these early blued magazines have just a couple of letters and numbers stamped on their spine and lower side. After a time, the finish was changed to black phosphate. Then the factory seems to have adopted an "O," stamped distinctively low on the spine's side, as a standard inspector stamp. Many of these "O"-marked magazines will also be found with a large "22" stamped on the spine.

Romanian magazines show incredibly little change over their long production history. New dies were clearly made to mimic earlier ones, and welding patterns remained consistent. They are sometimes derided for their very visible welds and poor finish. These issues are only cosmetic, however, and they function as well, and sometimes better, than steel magazines made by other countries.

Romanian semiauto AKs imported into the U.S. generally came with either a five- or 10-round shortened magazine. These differ slightly in length according to their capacity. It's interesting that the five-round magazine has a witness hole to show when it is fully loaded, but the 10-round magazine does not. Unfortunately, they were made simply by cutting down a regular 30-round magazine and forming crude lips for the floorplate to slide onto. Because some of the side ribs still remained on these new lips, removing or installing a floorplate generally requires a little effort. They retain the black phosphate finish of the larger 30-round military magazine. An examination of them clearly shows that the Romanian Cugir factory did not take special care when producing magazines for the commercial market.

CHINA

The Chinese started production of the AK-47 in 1956. The earliest Chinese AK-47/Type 56 magazine is generally referred to as the Sino-Soviet Model by collectors. The black phosphate body is of the First European Ribbed Type and has a blued floorplate. The defining difference is the use of a blued stepped follower instead of the oval-bulge-pattern follower found on European-type magazines. A check of the bottom rear of this magazine almost always shows a "66" in a triangle stamping that represents Factory 626 in the Hei Long Jing Province of China.

The second-pattern Chinese magazine, the Spine-Back Transitional, is a unique design. The body is similar to the earlier magazine, but lacks the three short horizontal ribs that wrap around the bottom back. The remaining two horizontal ribs, along the bottom side of the magazine, are much longer than normal and go from almost the very front to the very rear. Like the Sino-Soviet model, the body is phosphated, while the follower, floorplate and keeper are blued. The follower remains the Chinese stepped pattern. All the examples examined were unmarked, but its design is so unique that they are easy to pick out.

A third type of Chinese 30-round magazine was revealed during the Vietnam War that is called the Chinese Spineless by collectors. The magazine's two halves simply interlock and are then spot-welded together, thus eliminating the normal spine on the back. The ribbing pattern stamped into the sides remains the same as the earlier Chinese Spine-Back Transitional. This design is probably less expensive to make and weighs slightly less than other steel types—both important considerations when you're planning on making the millions of magazines that the Chinese have. Add in that they are actually easier to remove from webbing, grasp and insert in a rifle and you have an AK magazine probably seen in every post-1970 conflict featuring an AK. However, it is sometimes criticized because it is felt that the lack of a spine running down the back somehow weakens it, but in reality it has proven itself more than durable. Some of these made during the early 1990s, specifically for export to the U.S., will be found with "Made in China" stamped on the floorplate. A small number of these will be found with a unique stamped rear lug instead of the normal milled type.

The Chinese Poly Tech Corporation made special high-grade versions of the Chinese Spineless for commercial sale in the U.S. These Poly Tech Magazines generally show superior quality control when it comes to welding and bluing, have "Poly" and "China" stamped on their floorplates, and will have three witness holes in the back to show when 10, 20 and 30 rounds are loaded. At an additional cost, they were also available with a

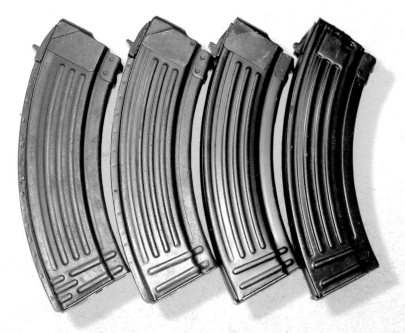

Chinese magazines (from left): Sino-Soviet, Spine-Back Transitional, Spineless and All-Stamped.

Twenty-round magazines (from left): Hungarian, Chinese Type 56C, Chinese Type 63 2+1, Chinese Type 63 2+2 Stamped Lips, Chinese Type 63 Black Plastic and Pro-Mag Coyote Tan.

chromed follower for easier cleaning and smoother function.

The Chinese continued to seek ways to cut cost while arming their huge and expanding military forces. Sometime, probably during the 1970s, they modified the Chinese Spineless to make it even faster and cheaper to produce. Called the Chinese All-Stamped by collectors, it eliminated the reinforcement plates welded to the top of the magazine and uses a stamped rear lug. The Chinese eliminated the need for the feed-lip reinforcement plates by stamping a pattern at the top that added both strength and tightened its fit in a rifle's magazine well. Only a few made it in direct from China before then-President Clinton sent a letter to the BATF, in May of 1994, outlawing imports of most Chinese guns and ammo. Large numbers of these once-rare magazines, however, were later imported from the former Yugoslavia starting in 2007.

The Chinese Norinco Corpora-

tion also produced a 30-round brown-polymer magazine, for the U.S. commercial market, meant to take advantage of the demand for the Russian AG4 plastic magazine. It was strengthened by having thin sheets of steel, as well as steel front and rear lugs, embedded within the polymer body. The follower, floorplate and keeper also remained of steel construction. These Chinese Phenolic magazines will be found with the Norinco trademark molded into the bottom left side and the "66" in a triangle factory marking on the bottom right side.

In 1991, the Chinese adopted a compact version of the AK, called the Type 56C, for use by their navy and internal security forces. Special 20-round magazines were issued with it that are basically just shortened versions of the regular Chinese Spineless magazine. Two versions of this magazine exist, apparently differing only in their rib patterns. The first has just three vertical ribs on its side, while the second has three vertical ribs and a single horizontal rib at the bottom. So far it appears that only a small quantity of the blued first-version magazine made it here

before importation stopped.

China produced a special five-round magazine for sale with its post-ban AKs meant for the U.S. market. Stamped with special dies, it has two vertical ribs and a single horizontal rib at the bottom. The Chinese five-round AK magazine uses the Chinese stepped follower, lacks a spine, is blued and has "China" stamped on the floorplate. "China" will be found stamped in two different sizes on the floorplate. Huge numbers of these were imported before the ban, and many dealers still have these NIW for sale.

The Chinese Norinco Corporation also attempted to make a more politically correct semiauto AK, for the U.S. market, called the NHM91. They put a rivet in the rifle's receiver, just behind the magazine well, that would only allow the insertion of a special five-round magazine with a milled cutout in its rear catch. This rivet was not required by any U.S. import restriction or law, and most rifle owners simply ground it down so any AK magazine would fit.

The NHM91 Five-Round is an easy magazine to identify. It has just three vertical ribs, has the rectangular milled cutout on top of the rear catch, lacks a spine, is blued and has the Chinese stepped follower. Interestingly, none of those examined had "China" stamped on the floorplate.

In the early 1960s, the Chinese military developed a select-fire carbine that combined features of both the AK and SKS and adopted it as the Type 63. Although little known in the West, it was made in large quantities by several factories. It was fed by a detachable 20-round magazine clearly developed from the AK's. However, its follower has a projection at its rear that travels up and down inside a special channel built into the body and activates the carbine's bolt hold-open mechanism when the magazine is empty. For some reason, probably due to the bolt hold-open mechanism, the stepped follower is reversed on a Type 63 magazine—the depression from which the last round is fed is on the left side. Because of this, the witness holes, indicating when 10 and 20 rounds are loaded, are also reversed to the rear left side. These Type 63 magazines were not designed for use in auto AKs, as they lack a milled clearance for the AK's disconnector on the right-side feed-lip reinforcement plate. However, they work just fine in semiauto AKs, but will block the bolt from closing after the last round is fired.

An impressive little collection can be made up solely of Type 63 magazines. At least five steel versions and one black plastic version have been identified. The steel magazines are centered around three basic body-stamping types: two vertical ribs with one horizontal rib at bottom (2+1), two vertical ribs with two horizontal ribs at bottom (2+2) and a very large star interrupting two vertical ribs with two horizontal ribs at the bottom. All three body types were made with the normal feed-lip reinforcement plates (as on a traditional AK magazine), but the last two types were also made with just ribs stamped to reinforce the feed lips (similar to the Chinese All-Stamped magazine).

NORTH KOREA

North Korea began manufacturing the AK-47 during the late 1950s as the Type 58. Little is known about its magazines, as they have never been directly imported to this country. The few 30-round magazines that have made it here are clearly copies of the Chinese Sino-Soviet, right down to the finish applied on them, and there is little doubt that they were manufactured with Chinese tooling and assistance. These can be identified by the North Korean arsenal's mark of a five-pointed star within a circle stamped on their spine.

YUGOSLAVIA

Yugoslavia's first AK, the M64, had a couple of unique features. It was built with a grenade launcher and a last-shot bolt hold-open mechanism. A notch cut into the upper left side of the M64 magazine activated the rifle's bolt hold-open mechanism with its follower, and a button on the left side of the receiver would release the bolt after a fresh mag was inserted. While the M64 corrected the AKs often-criticized lack of a bolt hold-open feature, it also created a greater problem in that normal AK magazines could not be used in it. This limited foreign sales and created possible internal supply issues.

The Yugoslavian M70 AK solved these issues in a simple way by making the magazine the bolt hold-open mechanism by itself. The Yugoslavians just omitted two small bumps on the inside of the magazine that stop the follower from traveling all the way up. In an empty M70 magazine, the follower is only stopped by the feed lips. A bolt returning, after the last round has been fired, will be stopped by the specially designed and strengthened follower that now blocks it. Using a Yugoslavian M70 magazine in any other AK will also cause the action to remain open after the last round is fired. It is believed that most M64 magazines were upgraded to this latter pattern by simply replacing their follower with the newer type.

The usefulness of the M70 magazine's bolt hold-open feature in combat is often debated, as once the empty magazine is removed, the bolt slams forward. Some users find it very useful as a range magazine. Checking that a rifle is empty and safe, as well as pushing a cleaning rod down the barrel, is far easier.

Yugoslavian M64/M70 magazines are easily distinguished from all others. Their blued bodies lack the short horizontal ribs that wrap around the bottom rear of the magazine, as found on all ribbed magazines except some Chinese models, and the two remaining long horizontal ribs stop well short of the magazines' front (unlike on the Chinese models). M64 magazines will also have their unique notch on the upper left side.

Examination of M70 magazines coming out of the former Yugoslavia shows two distinct variants. They are quickly differentiated by the shape of the witness hole in their back—round or triangular. Very notable differences in the follower and front catch will also be seen, as well as less distinctive differences in just about every other part. The general better condition of the Triangular Witness-Hole M70 Magazines, along with the fact that the earlier M64 magazines have round holes, has led to the probable conclusion that they are of newer manufacture. The lack of any transitional magazines, between the two types, would also seem to indicate production at two different factories.

There has been some speculation that the Triangular Witness-Hole M70 magazines were made in Iraq and provided as aid to the Muslim forces of Bosnia. However, no Triangular Witness-Hole magazines have been reported in Iraq. Most likely, the triangular M70 magazines were simply made at a second plant in Yugoslavia, set up to meet the demands of the Yugoslavian civil wars.

No shortened five- or 10-round magazines were made by the Yugoslavian factory for commercial sales in the U.S. rifles made after

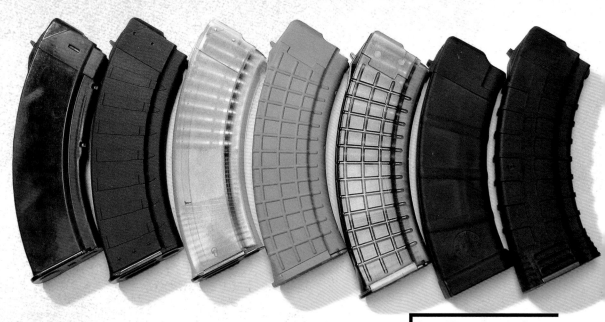

the 1989 ban, sold by Mitchell Arms, came with full-size 30-round magazines that were simply blocked to accept only five rounds.

BOSNIA

In 2006, in a large shipment from the now-dissolved country of Yugoslavia, came two newly discovered, but clearly related, 30-round magazines produced in what is now Bosnia. These magazines were made so that the bolt would be blocked by the follower after the last round is fired, and they were probably made under less than desirable conditions for the cutoff Bosnian forces. They are crudely stamped and welded, and poorly finished with what appears to be gray phosphate. Quality control clearly suffered on these, as a few of my magazines are too wide to insert into my Chinese-made AKs. Disassembly will also show that the plant making them relied on bent flat springs instead of the traditional coil spring. These magazines show both the ingenuity of the manufacturer and the desperation to arm the fledgling Bosnian forces.

Both Bosnian magazines are essentially the same, having only one wide, outward-facing vertical rib running down the side. The only real difference is the inclusion of a large stamped fluer-des-lis symbol on the bottom sides. The fluer-des-lis has special meaning to the Bosnian people and is included on their national flag. This symbol is also used by the Boy Scout organization, and this has led to this magazine being referred to by collectors as the Bosnian Boyscout. The magazine without the fluer-des-lis symbol is simply called the Bosnian Single Rib.

The so-called Bosnian Two-Rib 30-round steel magazines were also unknown in the U.S. until the above 2006 shipment. There is still, however, some speculation that they may actually be of Croatian origin. They appear to be what is claimed: another rushed expedient manufactured for an army cut off from outside supply. Most have a hastily applied blued finish, but a few also appear to have an equally poor phosphate finish. These magazines generally have rather poorly made followers, floorplates and keepers. There are two types of followers, unique to them, that are often poorly welded, one of which appears too short in length. The floorplates generally are poorly fitted and will often wobble side to side. The keepers are often oversize, thus making disassembly of the magazines difficult. Many of these also have a letter (W, X, etc.) and a number (2, 3, 5, 6, etc.) stamped on the bottom rear of the magazine.

There has been some speculation that the Bosnian Two-Rib was designed as a bolt hold-open magazine because it lacks the normal internal dimples that prevent a follower from traveling all the way up. Pulling an AK's bolt backward and releasing it on an empty magazine will usually result in the bolt being stopped by the follower. However, when firing the last round in a magazine, the greater returning force of the bolt invariably pushes down the follower so that the action will close. The traditional rounded end of the follower's bulge allows this to happen and also generally results in damage to the follower over time. The reason for making a magazine in such a way, other than to simplify production, escapes me.

In order to convert an imported rifle to a pre-ban configuration, or build such a rifle from an imported parts kit, a certain number of U.S.-made parts must be used. A U.S.-made magazine is an easy way to provide three such compliance parts: the body, the follower and the floorplate. This fact has spurred the U.S. development and production of AK magazines.

U.S.

A U.S. manufacturer, National Magazine, has been producing metal AK magazines since the ban was lifted. Taking the Chinese All-Stamped as a model, it stamps out the tops separately, then welds bodies of various lengths to these. Using this production model, it is able to produce magazines in an incredible variety of capacities. It produces mags in 10-, 20-, 30-, 40-, 50-, 75- and even 100-round capacities. As mentioned earlier, the end product strongly resembles a Chinese All-Stamped magazine, but the use of a green plastic follower and the welded joining of the upper and lower halves clearly differentiate them. No markings are found on these magazines, and they carry a glossy black enamel finish.

When Pro-Mag first introduced its U.S.-made polymer AK magazines, it only made a 30-round black version. These early magazines had thin-gauged 19-coil mag springs that were noticeably shorter than a Russian AG4's 22-coil mag spring. Failure to feed properly was a common problem with these early magazines. Pro-Mag increased the gauge and length of later springs, still with just 19 coil springs, on later production, and this has apparently solved the feeding problems. These magazines are also sometimes too long to fit in AKs, but the careful removal of a little material from the rear lug will solve this problem. Construction is entirely of polymer except for the steel spring.

Pro-Mag significantly increased its offerings in 2007. It now makes black, coyote tan and OD green magazines with capacities of five, 10, 20 and 30 rounds. It also makes clear and smoke-colored transparent magazines with a 30-round capacity. "PRO MAG" is prominently molded into the bottom left side of the magazine, as well as the floorplate. In a sign of the times, the company's Internet address is also molded into the floorplate.

An unexpected black synthetic 30-round magazine from Thermold Design & Development showed up on the market in 2007. These Thermold Magazines are marked "Master Molder" on both the right side and floorplate and carry the "Law & Gov't Use Only" warning on the left side from the high-capacity magazine-ban period. They are made from a durable nylon resin called Zytel and have three large horizontal ribs wrapping around both the sides and front. A very prominent and strong floorplate sticks out on the bottom. They are not generally considered an attractive magazine. Thermold's website shows that it also offers a 10-round version of the magazine, but I have been unable to find any distributors with them.

A quick examination will reveal that they lack an anti-tilt follower. Disassembly will further show that they use a spring not interchangeable with those from military AK magazines. On the plus side, the Zytel lugs look better designed, and more substantial, than those of a Pro-Mag. I also have had no problem inserting these in any of my rifles, and so far functioning has been 100 percent.

Tapco introduced its U.S.-made polymer 30-round magazine in the fall of 2008. This has a very distinctive ribbed pattern and an unusual flared-out bottom. "Tapco USA" is molded into the top left side of the magazine and the follower. The steel floorplate, the only steel in the magazine other than the spring, is also stamped "Tapco USA." The figures "7.62x39mm" will be found molded into the upper right side. Interestingly, a small date code and cage code number are also molded into the magazine. It produces these colored either black, dark earth or olive drab.

No trouble was experienced inserting these Tapco magazines into any of my AKs. The lugs, although polymer, appear strong, and the follower is of an anti-tilt design. They use standard AK-type springs, which actually appear to be stronger and longer than those found in many military magazines. Limited function testing showed 100 percent reliability. These would appear to be an excellent choice for the shooter needing a U.S.-made magazine.

OTHER AK MAGS

What is left out there to be discovered? Obviously, there are still some unidentified types. Hopefully, we will see some of the distinctive Romanian 20-round magazines carried by the dreaded "Securitate" in their compact AKMs during the 1989 Romanian revolution. Albania and Iran are reportedly making copies of the Chinese Spineless magazine. Iraq probably made a version of the Yugo M70 BHO magazine and some cut-down 20-round magazines. Cuba is probably making magazines that follow Russian patterns. North Korea certainly has made changes to its 30-round AK magazine over the years, and its soldiers have clearly been seen with 20-round magazines. There is also no doubt that there are several other countries that are making, or have made, magazines as well.

What are the best magazines for the shooter? It is hard to go wrong with any of the European Ribbed or Chinese steel types. The Bulgarian Waffle and Soviet AG4 magazines are excellent choices for those looking for military-quality synthetics, but they will cost you more. Some 20-round Hungarian or Chinese magazines will also prove helpful when shooting from a bench rest. The shooter needing U.S.-made magazines also has several good choices.

This is what most people think of when "7.62x39mm" is mentioned—inexpensive ball ammunition with poor terminal performance. With proper bullet selection, however, performance of this cartridge can be noticeably improved.

Improving

With an optic to replace the AK's terrible iron sights, this competition shooter engages targets out to 425 yards; his ammunition needs to be accurate enough to get the job done.

IT is sometimes hard to look past the most common loading to see a cartridge's full potential. The 7.62x39mm is a good example of this phenomenon. The ubiquitous military loadings of the 7.62x39mm were state-of-the-art in the 1940s but give lackluster performance today. In this article I'll describe three strengths of the cartridge which are largely ignored by its users: good performance in short-barreled rifles(SBR); the use of modern and heavy projectiles which have near ideal terminal performance; and heavy subsonic loads for suppressed use.

The popularity of the 7.62x39mm in the United States and the AK-47and SKS-based sporting rifles is based primarily on the historic rock-bottom prices of surplus ammunition. Within the last decade, cases of 7.62x39mm could be had for less than $100; however, today that price has risen by about 250 percent.

Although it is popular for simply blasting and plinking, the 7.62x39mm has ballistic value. The two old military loadings which dominate 7.6x39mm ammunition both use FMJ projectiles. The original Soviet M1943 load used a 123-grain FMJ boattail bullet with a large mild steel core.

In the 1960s the Yugoslavs decided to improve upon the Soviet load, and introduced their M67 ball loading. This differed from the Soviet load by being topped with a slightly shorter flat-base lead core FMJ. These changes were made to enhance terminal effects in tissue.

Chinese military ammunition in 7.62x39mm follows the Soviet pattern with a steel core and, like other Chinese ammunition, is banned from importation into the U.S. Standard mil-spec 7.62x39mm ammunition has a muzzle velocity of 2,329 fps with the 123-grain projectile.

Ballistics experts such as Dr. Gary K. Roberts (LCDR, USNR) have defined what "ideal" terminal effects look like from a quantitative standpoint. As a bullet enters a uniform tissue medium it creates a wound channel. This channel is conceptually split into several sections. As the bullet enters it continues straight and stabilized for some distance. This is called the initial upset depth, or the neck length. In this region, the bullet essentially creates a hole, more or less the same diameter of the bullet itself. At the end of the neck, the bullet starts to yaw, expand, or fragment and it creates a larger wound channel. This large wound cavity is defined by its length, height, and width. It's here where the most tissue damage occurs, as the bullet fragments split up and cause a lot of damage. At the end of this maximum damage cavity, the largest bullet fragment or fragments will continue creating a wound channel until they stop in the medium. This is the total depth of penetration.

Overall, the bullet pokes in the medium the "neck length" distance, then it expands, fragments, and/or yaws to create usually a football- or fan-shaped large internal wound. The largest fragments continue penetrating to the maximum penetration depth. Ideally, the initial upset depth is one inch or less; up to three inches is acceptable. The length of the maximum damage cavity should be as long as possible in the first 12 inches of penetration, and the cavity height and width should be as large as possible to ensure maximum damage. Finally, the total depth of the penetration should be ideally between 12 and 18 inches.

The wound channel produced by 7.62x39mm M43 FMJ-BT ammunition is far from this ideal. According to tests by Martin L. Fackler, M.D., its wound channel has an almost 10-inch neck. The bullet yaws and turns around to a backwards orientation causing a slightly larger internal wound for another nine to 10 inches, and then continues producing a thin wound channel for up to another 10 inches. Although the Yugoslav M67 load is slightly better in this regard, it still has a neck length of almost seven inches.

Compared to the experts' ideal wound profile, the 7.62x39mm fails all criteria. If we look at the 55-grain M193 and 62-grain M855 loadings of 5.56mm NATO, they have necks of approximately four

the 7.62x39

The performance of this 1943-vintage round can easily be improved.

By Zak Smith

The 7.62x39mm cartridge is very much a child of World War II. It's seen here with some of its peers, L to R: 9x19mm, 7.92x33 Kurz, 7.62x25mm, 7.62x39mm, 7.62x45mm, 5.56x45mm, 5.45x39mm.

A look inside a 7.62x39mm cartridge. Note the mild steel core in the sectioned projectile and Berdan primer in the cartridge case.

At close range, where the AK is most effective, accuracy may not be critical, but terminal effects are of utmost importance.

to five inches, maximum damage cavities four to six inches long and maximum penetration of 12 to 14 inches.

The 7.62x39mm's terminal ballistics using standard military ammunition are poor due to low muzzle velocity, the impact velocity is low, which prevents fragmentation. The bullet construction also has no features that aid bullet expansion or fragmentation. In short, standard military loadings in 7.62x39mm have terminal ballistics similar to small handgun rounds with non-expanding bullets.

However, the 7.62x39mm does have a redeeming quality: it penetrates intermediate barriers—such as thin metal or a chest-rig of loaded magazines—better than 5.56mm NATO. Just as the War On Terror was getting underway, the U.S. Army Special Operations Command created the Special Purpose Rifle-Variant (SPR-V) program to fill the need for a modular assault rifle capable of shooting 5.56 in addition to 7.62x39mm. This project was eventually cancelled, but

Special Forces soldiers had come to realize 7.62x39mm provided increased lethality over 5.56mm, especially when penetrating barriers. The Enhanced Rifle Cartridge (ERC) project followed, which created the 6.8x43mm SPC cartridge; however, that's another story.

From the drawing board, what can 7.62x39mm accomplish? With a case capacity of only 35.5 grains (the actual water capacity of the case), it has relatively little powder capacity versus its bore size. For comparison, the .308 Winchester has 56 grains of water capacity, while the .223 Remington has 30.9 grains. Even the .30-30 Winchester has a 45.0 grain capacity. If "overbore" cartridges have more than standard case capacity versus their bore size (such as magnums), the 7.62x39mm could be considered "underbore."

This underbore configuration leads to several intrinsic characteristics. First, ballistics are limited by powder volume. This means that not enough moderate or slow powder can fit in the case to produce

proper pressure and high velocity. Faster-burning powder must be used to produce rifle pressures; however, due to the burn rate, the velocity of medium and heavy projectiles will be limited. Second, lightweight projectiles that can be fired at high velocity will have ballistic coefficient (BC) values too low to retain a velocity advantage over much distance.

For example, if a lightweight bullet could go 300 fps faster than M43, but its BC was half the M43's FMJ, the 300 fps muzzle advantage would be lost by a range of even 100 yards. Thus, it's pointless to try to gain a lot of muzzle velocity at the expense of BC with 7.62x39mm. With modern powders, the military-standard 2,330 fps may be improved by 100 to 130 fps. Third, the 7.62x39mm will retain performance as the barrel length is reduced.

With these characteristics in mind, the 7.62x39mm is a good platform for launching medium and heavy .30 caliber projectiles at a somewhat sedate velocity. The standard loading of a 123-grain bullet at 2,330 fps represents what I believe ought to be the lower end of bullet mass used with the cartridge. In this bullet-weight class, terminal performance can be improved simply with the use of better bullets.

Unlike Western 7.62mm or .30 caliber cartridges, the Russian 7.62x39mm uses a non-standard bullet diameter: .310 inch (like the 7.62x54R) instead of .308. Thus most Western .30 caliber (.308) bullets are not ideal for use in the 7.62x39mm. This is slowly changing as a few bullet makers have come forth with modern bullets specifically for the 7.62x39mm.

The most interesting is the 123-grain Barnes TSX-BT. Barnes' TSX bullets are made from solid copper; they do not have a conventional jacket and core. The TSX bullet has a solid shank, and then a hollow-point nose. When the bullet impacts tissue, the hollow point expands to create a wide wound channel while the solid bottom shank stays solid for

A look at three sectioned projectiles, L to R: 7.62x54R light ball with mild steel core, 7.62x39mm M43 with mild steel core, 7.62x54R API with hardened steel core.

The 7.62x39mm M43 (R) was replaced in Russian service by the 5.45x39mm M74 (L). Note that both projectiles have a mild steel core topped by a lead filler.

Compared to the current "Big 3," the 7.62x39mm is less accurate, weighs more, and doesn't shoot as flat, but it throws a heavy slug. L to R: 5.45x39mm, 5.8x42mm, 5.56x45mm, 7.62x39mm. Photo courtesy of David M. Fortier.

Lapua's excellent support of the 7.62x39mm, offering both cases and projectiles, is no doubt due to Finland's military relationship with the cartridge.

Regular .308 caliber bullets are slightly undersize for 7.62x39mm; Barnes, Hornady, and Lapua are three manufacturers offering bullets specifically for the Russian cartridge.

excellent penetration. The TSX-BT bullet has a boattail to incrementally aid the BC value. Barnes TSX bullets have yielded impressive results on game from .22 caliber up to .33 caliber.

Standard lead-tipped hunting bullets such as the Hornady 123-grain SP will produce predictable results on game. Lapua has a 123-grain FMJ bullet that should produce terminal results about the same as the mil-spec FMJ. Standard construction hollowpoint bullets will produce more violent expansion and fragmentation, usually at the expense of overall penetration. Cor-Bon's 125-gr JHP and the Wolf Military Classic JHP both will provide increased terminal performance over standard FMJ. The Wolf JHP shows fragmentation in ballistic gelatin.

Here are potential untapped strengths of the 7.62x39mm. First, because of the relatively small powder-volume versus bore-size, relatively little performance is lost as barrel length is reduced. This makes the 7.62x39mm a perfect candidate for very short carbines. For example, a load that replicates M43 using Accurate #1680 powder will lose only about 70 fps when barrel length is reduced from 16 inches to 14 inches. Going down to a 12-inch barrel only loses another 83 fps, while a 10.5 inch barrel will still fire the 123-grain bullet at just over 2,100 fps. Thus the 7.62x39mm is an ideal cartridge for a short-barreled rifle, provided a bullet that produces good terminal ballistics is used.

The second untapped strength of 7.62x39mm is the use of heavier bullets. Although the vast majority of loads use a 120- to 125-grain bullet, a 150-grain bullet—the mainstay of .308 Winchester loads—can be fired at 2,100 to 2,200 fps from a 16-inch barrel. Going further, a 175- to 180-grain bullet can be fired at 1,900 to 2,000 fps. As bullet mass is increased, the ability for impressive penetration and terminal effects improves. These heavy bullets will lose even less velocity as barrel length is reduced. For example, a 180-grain load may lose only 100 fps as the barrel length is reduced from 16 to 12 inches.

Another untapped application of 7.62x39mm is to shoot medium and heavy bullets at subsonic velocity while suppressed. The best U.S. equivalent of this application is SSK Industries' .300 Whisper, also known by the non-proprietary near-identical equivalent .300 Fireball. Both of these are essentially shortened .223 Remington cases (actually .221 Fireball), necked up to .30 caliber. Slow pistol powders such as Hodgdon's H110 are typically used for these subsonic rifle loads. It is desirable to have limited case capacity: when there's just a little powder rattling around in a big case, ignition consistency suffers.

Instead of all the work required for a wildcat like .300 Whisper or .300 Fireball, the regular 7.62x39mm case can be used. It has a little more case capacity, but subsonic loads with fill ratios as high as 75 percent are certainly possible. With a 10-inch barrel and a short sound suppressor, a semi-automatic rifle in 7.62x39mm could be more compact than a regular 16-inch AK-47 but able to quietly thump 180- to 220-grain projectiles into anything within about 125 yards.

The accuracy of the 7.62x39mm has often been criticized. The primary reason is that neither the AK-47 nor the SKS rifles were designed for accuracy; they were designed for cheap manufacture, simplicity and reliability. Further, mil-spec 7.62x39mm typically has two to three MOA accuracy. With a good bolt action from CZ or another maker, MOA or sub-MOA results should be possible from handloads or Lapua factory ammunition.

So in summary, the 7.62x39mm cartridge's reputation is in some sense held hostage by the mil-spec ammunition that has flooded the market for years. Its terminal effects can be dramatically improved today by simply choosing a better bullet, such as the Barnes TSX-BT or other JHP. Although having a limited powder capacity compared to its bore size is usually thought of as a problem, 7.62x39mm is a good choice for SBRs and dedicated suppressed carbines. With modern technology applied to the 7.62x39mm as it has been to other cartridges, its capabilities and those of the AK platform can be transformed.

SOURCES ▐──▯

Barnes Bullets
www.barnesbullets.com

Hornady
(800) 338-3220
www.hornady.com

Lapua
www.lapua.com

ACCESSORIZE YOUR AK

TEXT AND PHOTOS BY DAVID M. FORTIER

Out of the box, your standard AK-pattern rifle needs little. Feed it decent ammo and clean it when you have the chance and it will serve you well. Items such as a sling and cleaning kit/combo tool usually are included, so you don't need to splurge here. Good-quality Com Bloc mags are readily available, and I highly recommend you put away at least 10 for your rifle. With these few items you are pretty much good to go. However, if you'd like to take your rifle into the 21st century there are some accessories you should seriously consider. A good flash suppressor, tactical light and red dot sight top my list. A flash suppressor, such as a Smith Enterprise Vortex, is easy to add and relatively inexpensive. The reduction in flash, especially with 7.62x39mm rifles, in low light is dramatic. This is money well spent.

Properly mounting a tactical light and red dot sight, however, can be a bit more difficult. One option that greatly simplifies things is Midwest Industries' AK-47/74 handguard. Although Midwest Industries is best known for its host of high-quality AR accessories, it has not ignored Mikhail's Avtomat. The company carefully considered what was needed and set about producing it at a relatively

If you'd like to mount accessories onto your AK, one solution is Midwest Industries' handguard system. It's easy to mount and priced right.

A tactical light and Aimpoint T-1 micro red dot sight were easily mounted to the WASR-10. No problems of any kind were experienced during testing. The handguard system performed as advertised.

affordable price. What they came up with is a very simple replacement fore-end and upper handguard. Machined from 6061 aluminum and then hardcoat anodized, both pieces feature T-marked mil-std 1913 rails. Manufactured here in the U.S., the unit allows accessories and red dot sights to be easily mounted. Plus, the whole system only weighs 10 ounces.

The only problem with fore-end rail systems designed for the AK platform is the lack of standardization among manufacturers. Midwest Industries got around this by making the design extremely simple. The fore-end bolts to the barrel, and the upper handguard bolts to the fore-end. Due to this, the whole system is very easy to install in just minutes using the included Allen wrenches. Once mounted, it is very secure, as long as you Loctite the screws. To see how Midwest Industries' offering would perform, I mounted it onto a Romanian 7.62x39mm WASR. No problems were experienced, and the installation only took a couple of minutes.

After the installation a KAC vertical grip and Pentagon light were mounted. The unit was then subjected to several months of use and abuse. I'm not a big fan of vertical grips on AKs, but I was interested to see if the torque would affect the fore-end. It didn't. Bouncing around in a vehicle didn't affect

SOURCE

Midwest Industries
262-896-6780
www.midwestindustriesinc.com

Manufactured from 6061 hardcoat anodized aluminum, Midwest Industries' handguard features mil-std 1913 rails.

it either. Neither did long strings of fire and the heat that accompanies such fun. The upper handguard is designed to mount a red dot sight, and I had no problems in this regard either. An Aimpoint Micro T-1 mounted easily, zeroed without incident and performed very well with no problems.

Price of a universal handguard system is $125, while a Yugo-specific unit runs $130. A Saiga-specific handguard is slightly more expensive at $135. Midwest Industries offers rails in not only black, but also flat dark earth and olive. If you'd like a red dot to go with your rail, the company offers a handguard/red dot sight combination as well. This combo comes with a Vortex red dot sight and retails for a mere $250.

The handguard bolts easily onto the rifle, and all tools are included. Note the numbered cross slots for mounting reference.

US PALM AK-47 ACCESSORIES

MAKING THE AK-47 MORE USER FRIENDLY. | BY DOUG LARSON

There is no way to count them all, but there are probably more AK-47-pattern guns around the globe than any other single firearm. They've been manufactured by countries worldwide and seen conflict everywhere—sometimes on both sides of the issue. There is no question that the gun is reliable, even when manufactured to specifications that are not up to the standards of the original Russian design.

AK variants are used by the U.S. military, law enforcement and, of course, by citizens to defend against aggressors. Even though the gun works nearly every time the trigger is pulled, it lacks many of the human interface features of modern firearms that make them easier to use. Ergonomics wasn't given much thought back in the 1940s when the AK-47 was created, and accessories for battle rifles pretty much stopped with cleaning kits and slings. But the people at U.S. Primary Armament Logistical Manufacturing specialize in making good equipment better by improving designs and building accessories that help the operator get the job done, so they figured they could make the AK-47 work better.

The young company that started in 2009 makes a variety of accessories and currently has five offerings aimed at the AK market. Rob Anderson, in charge of product development at US PALM, explained that the company constantly looks for ways to improve the usefulness of the AK class of weapons, but instead of manufacturing its own parts, it seeks out expert manufacturers and engineers with special abilities and then partners with them to finalize designs and have them make the product. Anderson realizes that no company or person has all the answers, but by forging relationships with the best designers and manufacturers, a superior product at a reasonable price can be brought to market.

Ideas come not only from staff who have law enforcement and military backgrounds, but also from real-life operators and instructors who are engaged in serious work every day. Once a design is completed and a prototype is available, staff, instructors and selected individuals test the equipment in the field. With feedback from these tests, US PALM makes any changes needed and then tests again. Something as simple as web gear can take months to finalize before it's ready for sale.

So what makes the company different from other accessory manufacturers? Anderson thinks it's the quality of the subcontractors US PALM partners with for design and manufacturing. "I'm very proud of the like-minded subcontractors we use who are focused on top quality and realize that the products we produce are used by people who risk their lives. We can't let those people down." Anderson went on to explain that the company is dedicated to developing and producing the world's finest firearms, weapons enhancements and accessories.

The only way dirt can get into the sealed AK30 box magazine is through the holes in the follower, but any dirt that does get in can be washed out with water. The magazine and spring resist rust and corrosion, and the exterior of the magazine has a slip-resistant surface.

AK30 MAGAZINE

The company's first offering was the AK30 magazine. Yup, a magazine for the AK-47. That's not too bright, some may say. After all, the world is swimming in 30-round AK-47 magazines—and they're cheap. However, many are also from manufacturers of unknown pedigree, so their reliability is questionable, and until the buyer actually tries them, it is not certain they'll work. If you've ever dropped your money on a gun show table to buy an AK magazine, walked away with the little gem and headed to the range only to find out the thing doesn't work and the vendor who sold it to you is long gone, you understand how important a reliable manufacturer that backs up its product can be. That alone could be a reason to buy the 30-round—or the 10-round version—AK30, but there's more. It's much lighter than the common steel magazine, which means a lot to an operator who is humping a full combat load. The polymer magazine body and follower won't rust— they're made of a special polymer— and the spring is corrosion resistant and designed to last without weakening.

Although the magazine cannot be disassembled for cleaning, any dirt that might find its way into the magazine through the small holes in the follower can be washed out with water. Additionally, the lower front edge is clipped at an angle, eliminating the sharp corner that sometimes gouges the operator's forearm. That's a nice touch. Even though the body is polymer, the locking lugs are steel, and the upper section is reinforced with a steel cage that presented a great many manufacturing challenges. The sides have a waffle pattern for increased strength and serrations along the front and back to provide a better gripping surface. Despite the texturing, the magazines easily slide in and out of magazine pouches, which are another US PALM product.

SPECIFICATIONS
AK30 MAGAZINE

CALIBER	7.62x39mm
CAPACITY	30 rds., 10 rds. available
MATERIAL	Proprietary polymer
OVERALL LENGTH	9 in.
OVERALL WIDTH	1³⁄₁₆ in.
WEIGHT	7.0 oz.; 7.4 oz. (10 rds.)
COLORS	Black, FDE, brown
FEATURES	Stainless steel latch cage
MSRP	$20

The AK Attack Rack features pouches to carry four AK-47 30-round and four double-stack pistol magazines. Supported by adjustable shoulder straps, this chest rig also has a large interior compartment for carrying other essential items.

AK ATTACK RACK

It used to be that magazine pouches resided on the operator's belt. That is often no longer the optimal place to put them, for a variety of reasons, a fact that US PALM acknowledges. After five months of development, Anderson and the crew came up with the AK Attack Rack, which is a chest rig sporting four pouches designed to securely stow 30-round magazines for quick access when needed. The pouches are curved to match the curve in the magazine, and the side that contacts the magazine's locking lug is lined with a smooth polymer insert to prevent the lug from snagging. The Rack also has four double-stack pistol magazine pouches and a large zippered compartment that opens from the top to reveal three additional pockets that can be used to stow even more magazines—perhaps stuffed with special loads or any other items the operator wants to have handy. The Rack is made of 500-Denier nylon by CSM Tactical Gear, one of the subcontractors that Anderson is so proud of. The Rack is secured by padded shoulder straps that cross the operator's back and really help when carrying a heavy load of ammo for a long time. There is also a waist strap that keeps the rig from flopping around during rigorous activity. All straps are completely adjustable, and there is even one-inch-wide webbing sewn to the back side of the Rack on which the operator can hang additional items.

I found that the Rack has plenty of room for gear, holds it securely and the pouches are roomy enough to carry magazines with the curve facing either direction without snagging. Why is this notable? Because you may find that grasping the reversed magazine with your palm outward and thumb down instead of with the palm toward your chest results in the magazine being properly oriented for a reload and your wrist doesn't have to be double-jointed in order to get a firm grip on the magazine during the draw. It's all personal preference, but either way works with the Rack. Other nice features are the adjustable straps that permit the operator to carry the rig high enough to clear any gear carried on the belt and low enough to permit easy withdrawal of magazines.

SPECIFICATIONS	
CAPACITY	4 AK and 4 pistol magazines
MATERIAL	500-Denier nylon
COLORS	Black, khaki, coyote, MultiCam, ranger green, OD green
FEATURES	Padded adjustable shoulder straps; large accessory pocket
MSRP	$135–$170

AK MOLLE POUCH

Recognizing that today's warfighter usually wears body armor and that wearing a chest rig is not always a good option when doing so, US PALM took what it learned from building the Attack Rack pouches and made AK30 MOLLE pouches that are attached to load-bearing equipment, using the MOLLE attachment method. These pouches are available in single or double configuration, and there is a triple pouch coming soon. Just like the Attack Rack pouches, each has a drain hole at the bottom in case the operating environment becomes more than just a little bit damp, and the retention device is an elasticized cord with a grab-tab that is quicker and a lot quieter than a Velcro flap. The pouches are light weight, made of durable 500-Denier nylon and can be attached to whatever MOLLE-compatible load-bearing equipment the operator is wearing. The sample pouches fit the magazines a bit tighter than the Rack pouches and could be made a bit roomier, though. My guess is that this will change on production pouches.

AK BATTLE GRIP

Another example of US PALM's efforts to make equipment that is operator friendly is the AK Battle Grip. The standard AK pistol grip is functional, but it's kind of like grabbing a one-by-two-inch stick. The polymer AK Battle Grip has slip-resistant texturing and is contoured so that it fits the hand and actually encourages the user to grasp the handle close to the receiver, which is better for rifle control. And where the standard pistol grip creates a corner at the junction with the receiver, the AK Battle Grip is rounded and much more comfortable. Inside the grip is a storage compartment that one can use for batteries or spare parts, and the water-resistant closure actually works without popping open when it shouldn't. The unit is easy to install and comes with the proper hardware to get the job done. If it looks familiar, it's because it's an adaptation of the AR Battlegrip made by another US PALM partner, TangoDown. Anderson reports that a lot of law enforcement officers and private military contractors are buying them.

SPECIFICATIONS
AK MOLLE POUCH

CAPACITY	1, 2 or 3 magazines
MATERIAL	500-Denier nylon
COLORS	MultiCam, coyote, ranger green, black
FEATURES	MOLLE compatible
MSRP	Starting at $10

Based on **AK Attack Rack magazine pouches, AK MOLLE Pouches can be attached to any MOLLE-compatible load-bearing equipment.**

SPECIFICATIONS
AK BATTLE GRIP

MATERIAL	Polymer
WEIGHT	5.8 oz.
COLORS	Black, FDE, brown
FEATURES	Water-tight storage compartment
MSRP	$20

The AK Battle Grip, which is made for US PALM by TangoDown, features a water-resistant compartment with a cover that stays put along with a comfortable profile that encourages a solid grip. The texturing reduces slippage even with wet hands.

AK TRI-RAIL

There's another product from US PALM that Anderson expects to be popular with those same buyers as well as friendly foreign military units. That's the AKTR or Tri-Rail. Looking around, US PALM noticed that Midwest Industries made a pretty good handguard rail system for the AK series of rifles, but it was lacking a good way to mount a red dot sight so that the sight would cowitness with the gun's iron sights. Anderson and his group bought a Midwest Industries rail system off the shelf and started cutting and welding until they finally were satisfied they had the right design. Midwest Industries thought it would work pretty well, too, so a deal was struck and now there is a topcover for the handguard rail system that puts a variety of optics, including the Trijicon RMR, Aimpoint Micro T-1 or H-1, or Leupold Deltapoint Reflex, at just the right height to co-witness with the irons. The unit sits high enough that air can get under it to cool things and prevent the sight from getting fried. Anderson told me that on a very hot Arizona afternoon he and the crew put nearly 1,300 rounds through a test rifle with no adverse effects on the sight and no loss of zero. Because there are so many AK variants, he can't guarantee that it will fit every one,

but it fit all of the many different test guns used. Since the unit is based on the Midwest Industries design, the topcovers can be purchased separately to retrofit existing rails.

I found that the Trijicon RMR fit perfectly on the Tri-Rail and greatly enhanced rapid target acquisition, making fast shots much easier. Because the unit puts a Picatinny rail at the six-o'clock position, it is possible to add a vertical foregrip to the AK, making the gun much easier to handle and control under recoil. By combining the Battle Grip, the Tri-Rail, a reflex sight and a fore-grip, the AK-47 becomes a much more user-friendly rifle.

If you are looking for accessories for your AK—or for any other firearm, for that matter—keep an eye on uspalm.com. The website is always revealing new products that are innovative or improve on an existing design.

SPECIFICATIONS AK TRI-RAIL	
MATERIAL	6061 aluminum
LENGTH	6 1/16 in.
WEIGHT WITHOUT OPTIC	11.5 oz.
COLORS	Black, others coming
MSRP	$125 full kit; $50 topcover only

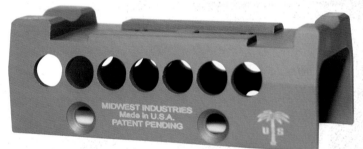

Easily attached to the AK-47-pattern rifle, the AK Tri-Rail that is a joint effort of Midwest Industries and US PALM, provides three 1913 rails for the attachment of various accessories and a topcover for mounting a variety of small optic such as this Aimpoint Micro.

MOUNTING A RED DOT ON YOUR AVTOMAT

By David Fortier

Photos by Sgt. Laura Fortier

Three ways to add a modern reflex sight to your AK.

ikhail's Avtomat has steadily grown in popularity with American shooters since the Chinese first flooded the U.S. market with cheap AK-47 rifles. Simple to use, rugged, reliable and inexpensive to shoot, the AK does indeed have a lot going for it.

Although not blessed with the accuracy of other designs, it's accurate enough for its intended purpose. What endeared it most to U.S. shooters, however, is its combination of utter reliability with a very affordable price. Here was a rifle your average blue-collar worker could easily afford—not just to buy, but to shoot as well. Plus, it could be counted on to work. No matter if it was fouled, dirty or fed cheap steel-case surplus, you could depend upon it to always go "bang." Refined and highly accurate? No, the AK is not the rifle to impress your peers with, but it's a design that can be counted on even under the worst of conditions.

When it comes to increasing the hit probability of any rifle, AK included, the simplest solution is to add a good optical sight. First proven in competition and then in actual combat, the modern red dot sight offers many practical advantages over traditional iron sights. Although the standard iron sights on an AK are certainly usable, a good red dot sight is both faster and easier to use. While some designs, like a flattop AR, are very optic-friendly, the AK is less so. This is due to its removable sheet metal topcover. So with the advantages of optical sights well proven, the question is: exactly how does one properly mount a red dot sight onto an AK?

Decades ago, when AK-47s first became commonly available in the U.S., the only optic mounts generally available were trash from China. Two types were common back then: top cover, and side mounts. The top cover mounts were cheap flimsy junk that thoughtfully adjusted your zero in-between shots. The most common Chinese side mount was a clunky design based upon the old Soviet M1891/30 Mosin-Nagant PU sniper side mount. In addition, some American companies caught a whiff of money to be made and turned out some horrible trash.

Times change, and today there are a number of excellent optic mounts available. What's interesting is the diversity in the designs themselves, and the ingenuity employed in their development. The three basic designs available that will best meet the needs of most shooters are the traditional com bloc side mount, Ultimak's gas tube mount, and LaRue Tactical's AK-IronDot.

Left: Have an AK and want to mount a red dot sight onto it? There are a number of good mounts available to make your installation easy. Below, left: A side mount is the easiest way to mount a red dot onto an AK, if your rifle already has the required rail. This IOR/Burris combination works well. Below, right: To use, you simply slide the side mount onto the rail and lock it in place with the throw lever. Installation and removal is quick and easy.

The Soviets developed their universal side rail system to allow night vision devices, like this 1PN-58, to be easily mounted onto Kalashnikov rifles.

The com bloc side rail is simply a short dovetail rail riveted to the rifle's receiver. This accepts a wide variety of day/night optics and optic mounts.

Com Bloc Side Mount

Perhaps the easiest optic mount to use is the traditional com bloc-type side mount. As its name suggests, this type of mount attaches to the side of the rifle's receiver via a corresponding dovetail base. This simple system was first developed by the Soviet Union to mate early night vision devices to its weapons.

The heart of the system is a short universal optics rail which is permanently attached to the left side of the rifle's receiver. This short side rail allowed the Soviets to easily mount either a day or night optic onto their standard combat rifle. Over time the rail dimensions were standardized throughout the Warsaw Pact countries. The result was a simple and durable universal rail system which could be used to mount magnified and non-magnified day optics as well as night vision devices onto a variety of weapons. As an example, a Soviet era night vision scope could be mounted onto any AK-47, RPK, AKM, AK74, RPK74, SVD or RPG7 that had a side rail.

The best feature of this attaching method is, it's simple and fast. To use, you merely slide an optic mount onto the rail and push it all the way forward until it stops. Then you rotate a locking lever clockwise until it's fully closed. To remove the optic, unlock the lever and pull the mount straight back off the rail. Zero retention is also fairly good. Removing and reinstalling the optic generally shifts POI less then one MOA, if at all. The downside to this system is that your rifle needs to have a side rail, and many AK rifles lack this feature. For the civilian shooter with an AK lacking the side rail—all is not lost. Side rails are readily available: K-VAR, for instance, is just one of many companies that offer them, and they are easily installed by any competent gunsmith.

If you wish to mount a red dot sight onto your AK, a side mount is one way to go. There are a number of good designs currently available from different sources. Kalinka Optics Warehouse has a number of designs that are produced either in Russia or former Soviet Republics. These range in price from $55.97 to $139.97.

K-VAR also offers a very robust mount called the KV-04. This is an improvement of one of their earlier mounts. Rugged and well designed, it features an aluminum rail, centered over the bore, that accepts standard Weaver rings. Suitable for use with both magnified optics and red dots, it attaches easily and locks into place with one throw lever. I have used this mount extensively for a number of years and have found it to reliably return to zero, or very close. Price of the KV-04 is $107.99.

The mount shown on these pages is an older one manufactured by IOR of Romania. Although no longer imported into the U.S., it is a good representative

example of mounts of this type. Mounted onto an Arsenal, Inc. 5.56x45mm SLR-106FR and topped with a Burris SpeedDot 135, it performed very well. The addition of the red dot provided a noticeable improvement in both speed and accuracy over the standard iron sights. This is especially evident when shooting on the move, when engaging multiple targets, or when shooting from awkward positions.

Side mounts do have some drawbacks that you should be aware of. One of these is that you cannot co-witness with the irons. You simply can't make a side mount low enough to do this. Plus, if the mount is rugged enough not to flex or bend, it adds a bit of weight and bulk to the rifle. In addition, if the rifle is equipped with a sidefolding stock, such as an AKS74 or AK74M, the optic must be removed in order to fold the stock. Lastly, if the mount is made to sit as low as possible—right over the top cover—it must be removed to clean the weapon.

The Burris SpeedDot 135-topped Arsenal SLR-106FR performed very well. The red dot added speed and practical accuracy to this well made 5.56mm AK.

Another option for mounting a red dot onto an AK is UltiMAK's AK mount. This is a simple and bulletproof mounting solution that works very well.

The UltiMAK AK mount replaces the standard AK gas tube and upper handguard. It bolts solidly to the weapon's barrel. Right: Unlike a side mount, the UltiMAK will allow a low mounted red dot, like this Aimpoint Micro T-1, to co-witness with the iron sights.

The traditional Russian solution to mounting optics on an AK, the side mount does have some positive attributes. While not perfect, it is one mounting solution to consider if your rifle is already equipped with a side rail.

UltiMAK AK Mount

Although the Russian side mount works well, it does have its drawbacks, not the least of which is that many AK-47 rifles lack the required mounting rail. Another solution to mounting a red dot sight on your AK comes from UltiMAK. A very simple and bulletproof design, the UltiMAK mount has become quite popular since its introduction for one reason: it works, and it works well. The mount itself is quite different from everything that came before it and demonstrates some very real out-of-the-box thinking by the engineers at UltiMAK. It consists of a simple tube that replaces the standard AK gas tube and upper handguard assembly. This is CNC-machined from aluminu, and has a MIL STD 1913 rail machined directly into its top. Two U-shaped retainers are used to lock it to the weapon's barrel to prevent movement. Good-looking and well made, it

When mated to a rugged optic, like this Aimpoint Micro T-1, the UltiMAK mount is almost as rugged as the basic Kalashnikov right itself. Practical accuracy is very good.

attaches easily to the weapon. Anyone who can fieldstrip their rifle can mount the UltiMAK in a couple of minutes.

UltiMAK's mount adds little, if any, weight to the weapon and zero extra bulk. Properly mounted, it provides a rock-solid platform to install an optic on. It's very rugged, durable and shrugs off abuse in the best Kalashnikov tradition. Not only that,

but it will even allow you to co-witness your iron sights if you carefully choose your red dot and rings. It's a very good unit, and it has seen quite a bit of professional use in both Iraq and Afghanistan.

I received a very early example a number of years ago, and mounted it onto a custom-built milled-receiver gun. I was pleased to note that it actually increased accuracy slightly on this particular rifle. I'm not an engineer, but as it was bolted solidly to the barrel I surmise it had a positive effect on the barrel harmonics. Average group size, using the iron sights, was reduced by approximately one MOA. Whether it will have this effect on your rifle I cannot say, but it did with my test rifle.

Topped with an Aimpoint T-1 Micro Red dot sight the UltiMak also allows me to co-witness the optic with the iron sights. So basically you have the best of both worlds. Normally you just use the red dot. However, if Murphy should throw a wrench at you and your optic goes down, your iron sights are clearly visible to save the day. Not only that, but the iron sights are fully usable throughout their adjustment range. I've shot this particular rifle at 600 yards using the iron sights with the optic mounted.

The optic never got in the way and the iron sights are fully usable just as they normally would be.

There is one point to be aware of using this mount, and that's heat. Unlike a receiver mount, the UltiMAK does heat up quite a bit. Although the mount itself simply acts as a guide for the gas piston, it is made of aluminum and attached directly to the barrel. So yes, it gets hot. That said, I have never had a problem using an Aimpoint Red dot sight with this mount. Over the years I have used this system extensively and fired thousands of rounds through it. All I can say is it works very well. I keep two rifles ready to go at my house, one is an AR, and the other is the AK seen here. Heavy use over the years has proven to me the UltiMAK is a rugged mounting solution that can be counted on.

In actual use the UltiMAK/Aimpoint T-1 combination works very well. The T-1 is a very rugged and compact little sight with a wide range of intensity settings. When put to work on the range the combination proved capable of making very fast and repeatable hits on steel. Although the 7.62x39mm test rifle has a short 14-inch barrel I was able to make consistent hits on LaRue sniper targets at 200 and 300 yards, shooting prone off the magazine. Off-the-bench, shooting paper at 100 yards, I averaged 2.5 inches for four five-shot groups. No problems of any kind have emerged with this particular mounting system.

All in all, the UltiMAK AK mount is very well made (probably better-made than most AK rifles out there). It's very simple to install, and extremely rugged. It will shrug

The newest AK red dot mount is LaRue Tactical's AK-IronDot. This combines a micro red dot sight and a fixed rear sight all in one neat package. Unlike other optic mounts, LaRue's AK-IronDot replaces the standard rear sight. Note the fixed rear sight for use if the optic fails. Photo courtesy LaRue Tactical.

off abuse that would dent a factory gas tube. An important positive feature is the ability to co-witness with the iron sights. Just be aware that this mount will get hot during prolonged strings of fire, choose your optic accordingly, and you are good to go. Price of the UltiMAK is a reasonable $98.

LaRue Tactical AK-IronDot

Although the name LaRue Tactical is very well respected among AR owners, the company has never catered to the AK crowd. This recently changed with the introduction of their AK-IronDot optic mount. Obviously designed using a clean sheet of paper, LaRue's offering is quite different from either the tradition side mount or UltiMAK's design. Very light, compact and simple, I suspect this mount is going to prove very popular.

I first caught wind of LaRue's mount a number of months ago during a visit to their facility in Texas. At this time their engineers were scratching their heads about just exactly how they were going to attach an optical sight onto an AK. Their goal was for a simple-yet-rugged mount,

which would be easily attached in the field. It needed to be low enough to co-witness with the factory iron sights. Also, it needed to mount a simple red dot sight to improve the hit probability of the rifle at commonly encountered engagement distances. In addition, it had to be affordable enough to be within reach of your average shooter.

Eventually LaRue Tactical hit upon the idea of using the mounting slot for the factory rear iron sight as an attachment point. By doing so they could make a very lightweight, simple mount that was low enough to co-witness with a replacement rear sight. In addition, it could be pivoted up enough to allow the top cover to be removed for routine maintenance. Using the concept of their popular AR-based IronDot as the foundation, the AK-IronDot was born.

The mount is fairly simple in concept and merely replaces the stock rear sight. The mount body is machined from steel and features a hardened steel rear sight blade/leaf spring. The base seats snugly down in the channel designed for the stock rear sight, allowing clearance between the

base and the receiver cover. Mounted onto the base is a Burris FastFire Micro red dot sight. This features a four-MOA dot with automatic brightness control via a forward-facing sensor. The sight is parallax-free at 50 yards, and is recoil-resistant to 1000 Gs. The lens is multi-coated, and it is powered by a common CR 2032 lithium battery. To better manage battery life, the sight has an on/off switch mounted on the side. Operating temperature of the sight is -10 to 130 degrees F. To protect the sight from impacts, an aluminum shroud covers the top. This has cutouts for access to the ballistic adjustments and on/off switch. Finish is a matte black, and the total weight of the mount and optic is less than 3.5 ounces.

The LaRue Tactical AK-IronDot is handsomely machined and very nicely made. Optic is Burris's FastFire red dot sight. Photo courtesy LaRue Tactical.

The AK-IronDot incorporates a protective shroud, similar to an EOTech, to protect the optic from impacts. Note the optic's power switch. Photo courtesy LaRue Tactical.

Out of the box LaRue's mount looked good, being nicely machined and well finished. It came with full instructions for the Burris FastFire sight, and adjusting tools. For this review I decided to mount it onto an older Krebs Custom AK-103K in 7.62x39mm. This is a fairly short (14-inch barrel), handy carbine that could benefit from a red dot sight.

To mount the unit you first need to remove your factory rear sight. This is accomplished by pressing down on its retaining leaf spring (a large screwdriver works well for this) and pulling the rear sight rearward out of its base. Next, simply hold the leaf spring down again and slide the mount into the rear sight base; let it rise up and lock into place. Then take the included rear sight/leaf spring and place it on the corresponding notched pins. Simply drive this to the rear (a hammer and punch do the trick) until it locks into place.

Once installed you need to check the zero on the iron sights and readjust these if necessary. I checked my zero at 25 yards and noticed both the elevation and windage were quite a bit out. So I adjusted the front sight for elevation, made a windage correction and fired at 100 yards. Since the rear sight is now fixed, you need to decide where you want your point of impact to be for your irons. Whether you decide to make it dead-on at 100 yards or slightly high for a 200-, 250-, or 300-yard battlesight is up to you.

Once I had my iron sights exactly where I wanted them, I adjusted the FastFire. To do this I simply moved the dot to the top of the front sight and then fired a group to confirm my zero. Adjusting the FastFire in this manner is quick and simple. The only thing to remember is to loosen the two adjustment locking screws prior to making corrections. After you make your adjustments, tighten the locking screws back down to make sure they don't shift.

With the optic mounted the iron sights co-witness in the lower third of the field of view. This allows an instant transition to the irons if the optic should fail. The main difference with this system is that both the front and rear iron sights are in front of the optic. The rear sight itself consists of a simple U notch that mimics the factory sight. Although the rear sight design is nothing special, it's quite adequate for its intended purpose. Shooting off the bench using inexpensive Wolf 122 grain FMJs, the short barrel AK-103K averaged 2.9 inches with both the irons and red dot. This was for four five-shot groups.

Moving to shooting drills on steel, LaRue's AK-IronDot performed very well. Using the red dot provided hits quite a bit faster than the factory iron sights. Moving to shooting at distance, the AK-IronDot again performed well. Shooting prone I was able to consistently hit LaRue Sniper targets (20.5 inches high and 11.5 inches wide) at 200 and 300 yards and frequently at 400 yards. All in all, performance was very good.

When I first saw this sight mount I was worried that a good side impact would send it for a loop. However, after installing it I can see that the AK sight base has two "ears" at the back that provide support. The EOTech like wrap around shroud also protects the sight itself from impacts. The design appears to be very robust. Plus, the mount can be pivoted up slightly to allow easy removal/installation of the weapon's top cover.

Regarding Burris' FastFire sight itself, I utilized it in varying light conditions and in total darkness—with no problems. The only issue I ran into was in darkness, such as in a house, looking out into a brightly lit area. Under such conditions the dot is fairly dim, but still usable. Another consideration is that the sight must be removed from its mount to change the battery. This, of course, is a less-than-desirable feature. Another thing to be aware of, like all red dot sights of similar design, is mud, snow

or dirt on top of the sight—which can block the projected dot.

Is this an optic I would choose for military or hard professional use? No. Will it serve most civilian shooters just fine? Yes. Although the mount will only currently interface with the Burris FastFire sight, other options will be available in the future. LaRue Tactical introduced this version first to provide an economical red dot solution for the average shooter. Price for the complete system, red dot included, is $285. Nicely made, well thought-out and quite innovative, LaRue's AK-IronDot is sure to become quite popular.

If you're looking to mount a red dot sight onto your AK rifle there are a number of good options available. Whether you choose a side mount, UltiMAK or AK-IronDot, make sure you practice with it. Consider taking a carbine course—and bring a friend with you.

SOURCES

Aimpoint
www.aimpoint.com

Arsenal Inc.
(702) 643-2220
www.arsenalinc.com

Burris
(888) 440-0244
www.burrisoptics.com

Kalinka Optics
(910) 202-4019
www.kalinkaoptics.com

Krebs Custom
(847) 487-7776
www.krebscustomAK47.com

K-VAR
(702) 364-8880
www.k-var.com

LaRue Tactical
(512) 259-1585
www.laruetactical.com

UltiMAK
(208) 883-4734
www.ultimak.com

Wolf Performance Ammunition
(888) 757-9653
www.wolfammo.com

MUZZLE ON IT

DEVICES FOR MINIMIZING FELT RECOIL AND FLASH ON A 7.62 AK.

BY BRIAN EDWARDS
PHOTOS BY SEAN UTLEY

The platform has been around for more than 60 years. Lately, there has been a surge in making products that can enhance the performance of the AK. However, one of the often-forgotten parts on any of these rifles is the one at the business end—the muzzle.

If your AK has a threaded muzzle, it may be possible to attach a device. State laws may dictate what you can or cannot add to the muzzle, so you must check the regulations. Some states still adhere to the details outlined in the federally imposed assault weapons ban that expired in 2004. For some, the best you can do is add a muzzle device.

Muzzle devices generally fall into three categories: muzzlebrakes, flash hiders and those that do both. For the purpose of this article I will be focusing on muzzle devices designed for the 7.62x39-chambered rifles. In spite of the increasing popularity of the 5.45, the 7.62x39 has been with us the longest and is still regarded as the standard for comparison.

SLANT COMPENSATOR

I started out with the traditional slant compensator. This is the most common muzzle device for the AK47, and as such, it's the least expensive. It has been on the AK47 since the 1950s on the AKM. With a retail price of about $10, it's by far the least expensive device you can add to your muzzle if you're starting out with nothing.

This compensator reflects the Russians' desire for something reasonably effective and inexpensive to manufacture. It's a tubular piece of steel that's been cut at a 45-degree angle, threaded and finished in a matte blue. It was designed to keep the AK somewhat controllable in full-auto fire by redirecting gas escaping at the muzzle, which pushes the muzzle down and to the left. This counters the tendency of the AK muzzle to follow the twist of the barrel and rise up and to the right.

MUZZLEBRAKES

Muzzlebrakes work by forcing the escaping gases behind a bullet to the side or in a rearward direction. This retards

The Flash Suppressing Compensator (FSC) is one of a series of muzzle devices manufactured for AK rifles in the U.S. by Primary Weapons Systems (PWS). The FSC series have been classified as a nonflash-suppressing device by the BATFE, which removes any restrictions in states that ban assault weapons.

muzzle rise somewhat. The better muzzlebrakes soften recoil and help the shooter recover faster between shots. A downside to many is that they often do nothing to reduce flash signature. Most tend to make the firearm a bit louder and uncomfortable for nearby shooters. On the upside, good muzzlebrakes put the shooter back on target, the importance of which cannot be overstated.

I obtained a small sample of U.S.-made muzzlebrakes. I chose U.S.-made brakes because they count as a 922(r) compliance part. They are also a breeze to install on an AK with a threaded muzzle.

KVar, Tapco and other U.S. manufacturers make a 7.62x39- variant of a brake that first appeared on the 5.45-chambered AK74 and has soldiered on with the AK100 series. It requires a more complicated machining process than the traditional slant compensator, hence its price is higher, usually around $50.

The AK100-style muzzlebrake features two square ports at the 3 and 9 o'clock positions, along

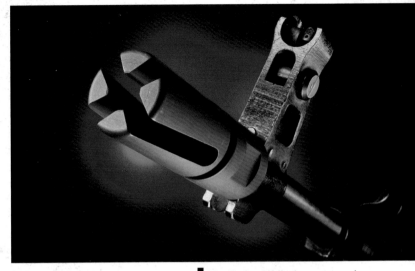

with ports at 11, 1 and 3 o'clock. This allows for an equal amount of gas to be expelled on both sides for braking, and escaping gas that is allowed to vent upward aids to counter muzzle rise. Unlike its older brother, the slant, this muzzlebrake is usually protected by a phosphate finish that offers some corrosion resistance. Many consider this the finest muzzlebrake to go on any general-issue rifle.

Primary Weapons Systems of Boise, Idaho, manufactures the J-Tac47. This is threaded for rifles with 14x1 thread pitch at the muzzle. At just two inches, it's relatively small and weighs just 2.4 ounces. The J-Tac47 is made of heat-treated 4140 steel with a Rockwell hardness of 56 and a zinc-phosphate Parkerized

finish. Included with the J-Tac47 is a small polymer washer to account for variances in threads on muzzles. The MSRP is on the high side of other muzzle devices that you'll find—$70.

The J-Tac47 has two J-shaped notches cut into the device at the 3 and 9 o'clock positions. Where the J curves, the notches are beveled to allow escaping gases to be directed rearward. This helps to dampen felt recoil. The straight portion of the J causes escaping gases to rise, helping to keep down the muzzle.

BRAKE COMPARISON
I enlisted the help of several shooters, ranging from new shooters to experienced ones. We met at a local range, and they fired multiple strings to form an opinion of felt recoil and muzzle-rise

The J-Tac47 is a highly effective muzzlebrake for AKs chambered in 7.62x39mm. It not only lessens the felt recoil, it does so without significant increase in blast noise directed toward the shooter or those next to the shooter.

reduction. The ammunition for this test was the 124-grain Ulyanovsk 8M3 JHP and the 123-grain V-Max from Hornady.

An unthreaded Romanian SAR1 was fired first to act as the control, and then the traditional slant compensator was mounted on a Steyr-imported Maadi. The slant offered nothing in the way of recoil reduction, and muzzle rise wasn't that noticably improved over the SAR1's unthreaded muzzle. It did offer a "look," so when you consider its price, no one minded.

Moving on to the muzzle-brakes, the American-made K-Var was mounted to a Saiga SGL21. The first comment was how noticably heavy the brake was. It is chunky, but each evaluator was impressed with its ability to dampen recoil. Some of the recoil reduction may be credited to the 90-degree front gas block, and some of it might be credited to its weight. The one thing that the AK74-style brake didn't do was control muzzle rise. Many didn't care for

the blast the brake produced. However, all agreed that it was better at reducing muzzle rise than the slant.

I threaded the PWS J-Tac muzzlebrake on a Hungarian SA85 next. It got some excellent comments from the participants with regard to recoil management. Some noticed a reduction in muzzle rise, while others didn't. Standing off to the side with a timer, I noticed that the J-Tac got everyone back on target faster. As with the AK74-style brake, nobody seemed especially pleased with the extra blast, but that's something with which one must deal.

FLASH HIDERS
Flash hiders (or flash suppressors, if you prefer) reduce a rifle's flash signature by quickly dissipating burning gases. Flash is frowned upon because it can inhibit the shooter's vision of a target in low-light conditions or give away a soldier's position on the battlefield.

And like U.S.-made muzzle-

brakes, U.S.-made flash suppressors also count as one U.S. 922(r)-compliant part. Of course, they are just as easy to install. Unfortunately, there may be restrictions in your jurisdiction that prohibit you from installing a flash suppressor on your AK. Some flash suppressors do a great job of reducing flash, while others do not. As with muzzle-brakes, I chose three flash suppressors that are all made in the U.S. and count as a 922(r) compliance part. In addition, they are all 14x1 threaded. I selected three for comparison that range from affordable to expensive, but as we all know, price doesn't dictate performance.

The Birdcage model from Cope's Distributing retails for $10, making it the most affordable flash hider of those tested. This unit was designed and manufactured here in the U.S. It's somewhat similar in appearance to the flash suppressor on the M16, but it's larger to account for the increased proportions of the 7.62 bullet that exits the barrel. The finish is matte blue, and at 1¾ inches, it's the shortest flash suppressor tested. It also ties for the lightest, weighing just 1.9 ounces.

The Cope's Birdcage has a fairly simple approach. At the rear are three separate front sight tower detent cuts. All three are set to have the cuts on either side. This is so that any flash is kept out of the shooter's line of sight. Surrounding the device, the birdcage features six long cuts with a slight bevel at the end of each and, just like the AR-style birdcage, the end is cleanly rounded off.

Smith Enterprise Vortex

PWS FSC47

Liberty Cans Phoenix

Cope's Birdcage

PWS J-Tac47

Using the rifles with the 124-grain Uly 8M3 surplus load, the camera captured varying degrees of flash signature. Each flash hider lived up to its description with the 123-grain load from Hornady.

IN SIGHT WITH XS SIGHTS
BY BRIAN TINDLE

The XS tritium stripe offers you a front sight that is easy to pick up in all lighting conditions. You can use your stock rear, just opened up a bit.

The AK wasn't designed to be a match-accurate rifle, so match-quality sights were never a consideration. AK sights function to put bullets on targets at reasonable combat distances, and they do just that.

While certainly usable, the standard sights on the AK can be improved. That's exactly what XS Sights of Ft. Worth, Texas, has done. It didn't stop with one option; it has given the AK aftermarket three ways to improve the shooter's ability to put rounds on target quickly and accurately.

The lineup starts with a 24/7 tritium post. This post replaces the standard black post and the drum. The XS sight features a vertical tritium tube set inside a larger white ring (almost an oval). In the daytime, it's this ring that really stands to attention, and at night, the vertical tritium post gives off a strong green glow. It's a fast-acquiring sight and can be used with a standard rear leaf sight as long as you don't mind opening up the notch a bit. The XS sight installation kit comes with the post, drum, set screw, Allen wrench, delrin sight tool, punch and Loctite.

The XS tritium post is very easy to install. Simply remove the original front sight post, then the drum. Before installing the new drum, make sure the set screw is not in. Then, using the supplied punch, begin firm strikes with a small hammer. Make certain that the sight pusher is not facing the drilled and tapped side of the drum. With the drum in place, screw the front sight into it and begin sighting in your AK. Keep in mind that the tritium faces one direction. There's no reason for it to serve as a target indicator when you're up against a threat. Once you're sighted in, add a dab of Loctite to the set screw and, using the supplied Allen wrench, screw it in. The set screw prevents the sight from rotating under recoil.

A second offering from XS Sights is the 24/7 Big Dot. This sight is born from the XS pistol sight lineup. The rear sight is similar to the standard AK rear in installation, but that's where the similarities end. It uses a phosphate-coated steel plank that is dovetailed for a Colt 1911 rear. The rear sight uses a plain white vertical bar. There is a small set screw positioned toward the rear that requires careful attention. The front sight is the signature Big Dot, a green tritium tube enshrined in a large white ring. This gives the shooter the ability to pick up the front sight in bright-, low- or no-light situations. Installation is similar to the aforementioned post except that it is wise to use the provided delrin sight tool to screw the sight into the drum. A word from experience: Use the supplied instructions, and follow them to the letter.

Finally, XS has acknowledged that there are some who would rather use the 24/7 Big Dot as a stand-alone sight or in conjunction with another rear sight. The company doesn't recommend this, but it's an option should you desire it.

American ingenuity is showing again that we can take a good thing—or in the case of the Avtomat Kalashnikov, a great thing—and make it better. XS Sight Systems saw the demand and answered it.

SOURCE
XS Sight Systems
888-744-4880
xssights.com

The Liberty Phoenix flash suppressor is a moderately priced unit that can usually be found for about $40. I was introduced to the Liberty Phoenix by Paul Gomez of Tactical Response. Measuring 2¼ inches, this device is longer than the birdcage type, but its weight is identical at 1.9 ounces. The finish is more of a matte gray, which is still nonreflective and pleasing. The Liberty Phoenix flash suppressor has four slanted ports that are each cut bi-directionally, allowing flash and gas to escape in three ways: up, down and forward. The ribbing helps reduce small vibrations when the rifle is fired. Of note, with this unit you can still attach a bayonet.

A popular muzzle device with our troops is the Smith Enterprise Vortex. This design has been adapted to everything from the M14 to the M2 .50-caliber machine gun. The company does not refer to the Vortex series as flash suppressors, but rather flash eliminators. This is the biggest and heaviest of our dedicated flash suppressors. It is 2½ inches in length and weighs 3.7 ounces. The Vortex has a tough, Parkerized finish that stands up to corrosive ammo. Its price runs on the high side of the flash suppressor category, the AK model usually found for sale at $105.

The Vortex uses SEI's patented 15-degree helix design. The four slanted ports are each cut bi-directionally, which allows gases to escape in two directions. A plus to this design is that it's self-tightening. Why is this a big deal to AK enthusiasts? Not all AKs have a detent pin in the front sight tower (think the Romanian SAR series). Another bonus to the Vortex is that it will allow for the use of SEI DC sound suppressors.

HIDER COMPARISON

For the range evaluation, I kept the same type of ammunition used in the brake comparison and maintained the unthreaded Romanian SAR1 as our control. My group fired a few of each round to get an idea of what can be expected in terms of flash suppression. The results were interesting. The 124-grain Uly 8m3 JHP erupted as expected, but the Hornady round presented very little flash.

I threaded the Cope's Birdcage flash suppressor onto the barrel of an SA85 and fired. I noted that the flash of the Uly round was reduced quite a bit. It was still there, but nowhere near as noticeable as an AK without it. It would be safe to say that it offered a 60 percent reduction in flash signature. On the other hand, the Hornady round presented virtually no flash, with only a dull yellow signature appearing within the device itself. Not bad for a $10 investment.

The J-Tac47 features cuts at the 3 and 9 o'clock positions in the shape of the letter J to compensate for felt recoil. The kit includes a high-heat polymer washer for AKs that need a spacer between the front sight base and the compensator.

All muzzle devices evaluated were manufactured in the U.S. The birdcage-style flash hider attached to the muzzle of this AK is from Cope's Distributing. The other flash hiders are (from top to bottom) Smith Enterprise Vortex, PWS FSC47, PWS J-Tac47 and the Phoenix from Liberty Cans.

The Liberty Phoenix was attached to the Steyr-imported Maadi. The Phoenix almost negated all of the flash from the Uly JHP. I say "almost" because within the device itself, the appearance of a faint yellow flash could be seen, but nothing escaped. The Hornady round produced no flash whatsoever. In fact, we fired a few more rounds to check ourselves with the same conclusion.

The final flash suppressor— sorry, flash eliminator—tested was the Vortex. The Vortex was attached to the SA85. The Uly JHP offered nothing in the way of flash. I had the shooter fire more Uly, and only once did I get a small spark. Very impressive. Like with the Liberty Phoenix, there was absolutely no flash. In keeping with the results found using Hornady in earlier comparisons, testing the Vortex with the Hornady load lived up to the flash-eliminating description offered by Smith Enterprise. We were wasting ammo trying to detect flash with this combination.

DUAL PURPOSE

The final category with regard to muzzle devices is the ones that function as both muzzlebrakes and flash hiders. They aren't typically the best at being a muzzlebrake, nor are they the best at suppressing flash. They do, however, perform both functions to an acceptable degree.

As this category is relatively new, there is only one offering for AKs at this time: the FSC47. Like the J-Tac47, it comes from Primary Weapons Systems and is made of hardened 4140 steel tested to a Rockwell hardness of 56. Also like the J-Tac47, the finish is a zinc-phosphate Parkerizing that is not only durable, it oozes quality. The FSC47 includes a small polymer washer to make up for incorrectly threaded muzzles and costs $100.

The brake aspect of the FSC47 functions with cuts that remind one of fish gills—two on each side located at the 3 and 9 o'clock positions. These gills face back in the direction of the shooter and are directionally cut upward to compensate for muzzle rise. Remaining gases are dissipated by a four-prong flash suppressor where each prong is bi-directionally cut.

When I attached this combination device, I did so with the understanding that it should be a jack of all trades, master of none. However, on the range it actually proved to work exceptionally at both functions. With the FSC47 attached to the Steyr-imported Maadi, many of the shooters found that it was similar in performance to

The Phoenix flash hider for AKs has bi-directional ports cut around the perimeter to assist in the leaning of the air/fuel mixture that is required for combustion. The small grooves cut around the perimeter of the ports are for anti-resonance and help to reduce barrel vibrations and stabilize the bullet sooner in flight.

the J-Tac brake from the same company. In a darkened indoor range, its flash-suppressing capabilities were just a bit better than the Cope's Birdcage. With Uly-loaded Wolf ammunition, flash was noticeable, with small streaks escaping beyond the muzzle. The Hornady revealed minimal flash, obviously a trend that was consistent with this load.

Which should you choose?

What's right for one person may not be right for another, but the options are out there. When it comes to AKs, so many of our decisions are influenced by style. And each of these offers something for everyone.

SOURCES

Cope's Distributing
866-523-2673
copesdistributing.com

Hornady
800-338-3220
hornady.com

K-Var
702-364-8880
k-var.com

Liberty Cans
706-661-6911
libertycans.net

Primary Weapons Systems
208-344-5217
primaryweapons.com

Smith Enterprise Inc.
480-964-1818
smithenterprise.com

Tapco
800-554-1445
tapco.com

Wolf Ammunition
888-757-9653
wolfammo.com

PART IV
BUILDING AND TRAINING

CALIFORNIA LEGAL

HOW A CALIFORNIA RESIDENT CAN LEGALLY OWN AN AK VARIANT.

BY TIMOTHY YAN

Californians can't have an AK." That statement is just a myth. While the state's policies tend to restrict private gun ownership and attempt to ban rifles resembling those that are used by various militaries, the Calguns Foundation, the Second Amendment Foundation and many other California gun rights organizations have fought back. If you're a California resident, you can legally own an AK-style rifle if it wears certain modifications. This article is focused mostly on AKs for Californians, but the information could be useful for residents living in states with similar restrictions.

the legal flow of AKs and effectively create a market vacuum. The economy is bad, but the average California shooting enthusiast still has enough disposable income to spend on a new gun. Thankfully, Arsenal Inc. is now offering California-legal AK models to Golden State residents.

You don't have to buy one of those pre-made California-compliant models. You can do the conversion yourself on just about any make and model. Before you buy one, you must check the AK and AR-15-series rifle ban list with the California Department of Justice. Fortunately, almost everything on that list is old models manufactured before 2001.

Next, you need to get an AK legally transferred to a California FFL holder. There are a lot of uninformed Californian dealers out there, so you should find one who specializes in transferring lower receivers and black rifles. For private sale, the seller can ship the gun directly to your local FFL. If the gun is shipped by an FFL, he must have a registration with the California Firearms Licensee Check System (CFLC), and he needs to obtain a Firearms Shipment Approval letter to be shipped with the gun. This is actually a very simple process for the FFL holder. All it takes is a few minutes online and a printer to print out the shipping letter.

This converted Krebs Custom AK74 abides by California gun laws and looks very similar to a normal AK that citizens can lawfully own in nonrestricted states.

GOLDEN

I stopped by a booth at SHOT Show a few years ago and talked to company representatives about making a California-compliant AK model. The floor manager wasn't interested. The federal assault weapons ban had expired and business was thriving.

Panic buying is long gone, and the gun market is now saturated with AKs and other black rifles, except for one place: California. The state's anti-gun laws hold back

Before an AK can be shipped, the rifle has to be in a California-legal configuration. The easy way to do this is to take off the pistol grip and dissemble all the high-capacity magazines. Now both the gun and the magazines are legally considered parts. For my project, I obtained a Krebs Custom AK74 built on an EAA-imported Izhmash receiver and transferred it into California following the aforementioned process.

After I picked up my Krebs AK74 from my FFL, I was looking for a way to convert it into a California-compliant rifle. I was introduced to Mike Addis of Solar Tactical in Hayward, California (solartactical.com). I hit it off with him immediately since we are both ex-Marines. After he left the Corps, he went on

A closer look at the AK magazine lock from Solar Tactical.

To use the rapid-reload tool, fit it into the slot on the underside of the Solar Tactical magazine lock, then push the attached magazine forward.

to Iraq as a private military contractor (PMC), and he tells me that the AK was his primary carry gun while working in the Sandbox. Mike told me that his truck gun was Kalashnikov's

other famous creation, the PKM. The captured belt-fed machine gun had most of its stock and barrel cropped off, so he used the 7.62x54R MG for protection outside the truck window.

The author's converted, California-compliant AK74 works and handles just fine at the range.

It only took a few minutes to install the magazine lock on this AK74.

The Kydex magazine insert seats between the spring and the rear of the magazine interior. It functions as a limiter to stop the follower from going down beyond the legal capacity limit.

SOLAR TACTICAL

Solar Tactical was started by Mike Addis more than two years ago between his PMC rotations. When he was back home, he wanted to train with the AK to keep up his fighting skills. Due to the state's restrictions, he was looking for compliant parts but was frustrated with the available options on the market. They were either hard to install or required permanent modification to the gun, so he started to develop his own compliant parts for his AKs. His current products include the magazine lock, 10-round magazine conversion kit, rapid-reload tool and a featureless grip.

Installing Solar Tactical's AK magazine lock is a simple affair. It clamps on to the triggerguard and is fixed in place by four small screws. The longer adjustment crossbolt is for getting the proper fit on different AK variants. The only tool needed is a small Allen wrench, and it's recommended to use some Loctite on the screws. The device completely covers the magazine release, as is required by the law. According to the law, the magazine has to be nonmoveable. There's a slot opening at the bottom where the user can insert a tool and press the magazine release. Using a tool to take out the magazine is considered dissembling the rifle. The tool could be a screwdriver or just the tip of a bullet, which is where the term "bullet button" came from, a term that sometimes is synonymous with a compliant magazine lock that features a tool access hole to the magazine release.

The precut 10-round magazine insert by Solar Tactical was used to convert this high-cap magazine part kits into a low-cap 10-rounder.

The combination of the rapid-reload tool and the Solar Tactical magazine lock allows the user to do magazine changes as fast as on a regular AK–almost.

Solar Tactical offers a companion AK rapid-reload tool for its magazine lock. It consists of a protruding, plastic-covered metal peg that, once installed, is attached to the side of the magazine body by a removable hook-and-loop strap. To use it, just hold the magazine sideways and place it under the triggerguard with the peg pointing up. Insert the peg into the opening slot under the Solar Tactical magazine lock then hit it forward with some force to push on the magazine release and knock out the inserted magazine. The carefully designed angled bottom on the magazine lock aids the process.

High-capacity magazines can be converted into 10-rounders by using the Solar Tactical 10-round magazine insert conversion kit. Just put the precut Kydex insert between the rear interior of the magazine body and the spring. The flexible Kydex material allows the insert to curve with the magazine's contour. Legally, the converted magazine has to not be easily converted back to high capacity. The simplest way to do that is by fixing the magazine floorplate to the magazine body with epoxy or a screw. I found Solar Tactical inserts to be superior to any other magazine conversion methods and products out there.

Last, as an alternative to using the magazine lock, you can do a so-called featureless conversion. Solar Tactical sells a featureless slip-on Kydex grip that, when installed on the pistol grip, removes the pistol grip as a restricted feature. While it looks goofy, the slip-on Kydex grip actually works better than I expected. Another benefit of this method is that it is then legal to use high-capacity magazines with the rifle.

ACTIVE-DUTY MEMBERS
So, you're in the military and you just got the order to relocate to California. Don't panic just yet. You can legally bring your AK with you. The active-duty military member's right to bear arms is protected under the Servicemembers Civil Relief Act, formerly known as the Soldier's and Sailor's

The Kydex slip-on, featureless grip (right) is shown beside the installed magazine lock (left). It's legal in California to use high-capacity magazines with a featureless build.

Relief Act. The intent of the law is that, while the serviceman may physically live in a restricted state like California because it's his assigned duty station, under federal law he still legally resides in his home state, which may not carry the same restrictions. Therefore, the local California or other restricted state's gun laws largely do not apply to him. There are still some limitations to this exemption. In California, the 10-round magazine capacity restriction still applies, and the owner can't transfer his noncompliant guns to any local resident. When a serviceman is discharged or retired from the military, his noncompliant firearms must be transferred out of the state. The owner also has to apply for the California

Special Weapon Permit for active-duty military through the sheriff's office closest to his new duty station prior. After that, the guns must be transferred in through an FFL. For detailed information on the Special Weapon Permit, call the California DOJ Bureau of Firearms.

All of the above won't work for those servicemen who are native Californians. The work-around would be to change resident status to another state. Once this is done, the serviceman can apply for a Special Weapon Permit like anyone else. I did this when I was stationed at Camp Pendleton. For me, the same issue applied. When I got out of the military, any gun that I acquired through the Special Weapon Permit didn't stay in California.

SOURCES

Calguns Foundation
calgunsfoundation.org
calguns.net

California DOJs
Bureau of Firearms
ag.ca.gov/firearms
916-227-7527

California Firearms Licensee Check System (CFLC)
caag.state.ca.us/firearms/forms/pdf/cflcapp.pdf

CFLC online shipping letter request
cflc.doj.ca.gov

Solar Tactical
925-447-4743
solartactical.com

BUILDING THE ACCURATE
KALASHNIKOV
SHOOTER

BY GABE SUAREZ

PRECISION IS MORE THAN A QUALITY RIFLE AND SCOPE.

The Kalashnikov is here to stay in America, sometimes to the gnashing of traditional teeth that insist it's not capable of what a rifle should be capable of. Specifically, of course, some insist the rifle is simply not accurate. Well, nothing could be further from the truth. At several recent Kalashnikov Rifle Gunfighting classes at my school, Suarez International (suarezinternational.com), we have added a long-range component to the training because, while CQB shooting is fun and easy to learn and apply (by both trainer and trainee), the AK is in fact a rifle and should be used as such. Many training courses seem to focus exclusively on the CQB realm, and thus the trainee never learns actual riflery, but rather what we might call "submachine gunnery." I want our students to leave class skilled as complete riflemen.

We need to kill the notion that the Kalashnikov rifle is inaccurate. It is quite accurate if the shooter understands how to properly utilize it. The original Sturmgewehr concept required, among other things, the capability to strike point targets out to 300 meters. Wehrmacht studies (later learned by the Soviets as well) had shown that the majority of engagements occurred inside 300 meters.

One may argue how some calibers can reach farther, etc., but the truth of the matter is that in the field (different from the known-distance range with white-painted targets), human beings are quite difficult to see beyond 300 yards—a fact both the Germans and Russians learned in World War II.

The elements of the standing position include cheekweld, proper placement of the rifle in the shoulder and a desire to be as relaxed as possible.

The kneeling position allows the shooter to lower his profile and get steadier than the standing position allows.

The fact that one cartridge can shoot well past that distance is irrelevant when one cannot see or identify the enemy farther than that. Thus optimizing the assault rifle for that general range makes perfect sense. According to operational snipers I have debriefed, most sniper shots are taken at or just outside that range, meaning that most infantry rifle shots are taken well inside that range. The problem is that students of the rifle tend to get caught up in the minutiae of calibers and groups and forget the point of the exercise.

To hit at the ranges discussed, and a little beyond, we need an accurate rifle. Making the Kalashnikov into an accurate rifle is technically easy, given new parts, a new barrel, proper assembly and a suitable optical sight. But the telling point regardless of how accurate a rifle you have will be your understanding of the fundamentals of rifle marksmanship. At our recent Red October series we had a gourmet chef in our class who had barely learned how to operate his AK, yet he made repeated hits on steel at 200 yards with an understanding of these time-proven principles. They applied

one on top of the other in this exact order. Here are the secrets.

POSITION—The rifle is held at four points of contact (sometimes five with a rest), with the firing hand, the support hand, pulled into the shoulder and with the cheek firmly on the stock, giving you a uniform view of the sights.

CHEEKWELD—Consistent sighting (with irons or optics) begins with proper cheekweld, positioning the cheek at the same place each time on the stock. Besides before and after placement of the weld, it also determines the height of the eyes in relation to the sights or scope. Many experienced and advanced students who come to us have, amazingly, never learned about cheekweld.

NATURAL POINT OF AIM—The optimal position of the body in any shooting position, whereby, at rest, the sights will still line up with the intended target. NPOA can be checked by closing both eyes, breathing and relaxing. When the eyes are opened, the sight picture should remain unchanged. If not, adjust the body (not just the rifle) as necessary.

SIGHT ALIGNMENT—On the AK rifle, the sights are basically the same as on your handgun. Front post—rear notch. Align them as you do your pistol. I am a great fan of electronic sights over the irons. If you were nearsighted, nobody would sneer at you for buying glasses, but the AK crowd seems to have an aversion to technology that is astounding. If you cannot see your sights, put a scope on your rifle just as every single U.S. soldier has done. With optics, alignment is obtained when there is no shadow at any point in the circumference of the field of view.

SIGHT PICTURE—Sight picture is the placement of the aligned sights in relation to the target. Sight picture is greatly enhanced by closing the non-shooting eye while refining the sight picture. I laugh when guys tell me they keep both eyes open for a 300-yard shot. Close the nonshooting eye and your life will become considerably less complicated.

BREATH CONTROL—Oxygen deficit or holding your breath leads to an unsteady hold, as the muscles require more oxygen. Therefore, the trigger should be

The sitting position offers far more potential for accuracy than either standing or kneeling.

The prone position is the king of accuracy. Get in line with the rifle, as flat and low as possible.

pressed at a point in the respiration cycle (respiratory pause) when the shooter is steadiest. Inhale and exhale normally, and when the air feels like it has been expelled, you enter the respiratory pause. This is about six to 10 seconds where you can press the shot.

TRIGGER CONTROL—Trigger control is the most important area, and it's where most shooters fail. The "finger off the trigger" mantra has created a generation of shooters afraid of their triggers, and they pop that digit off the trigger like a burned hand off a skillet as soon as the shot goes off. Regardless of who has taught you that, it is wrong. A perfect break results from steady and even pressure straight to the rear until that pressure suffices to release the trigger mechanism. Forcing it will lead to failure.

FOLLOW THROUGH AND RESET—This means that you reestablish everything at the moment before the shot discharged. During the shot, change nothing. Let me repeat: Change nothing. Leave your hold as is and your face on the stock. Focus visually on the sights/ scope as the shot leaves the rifle, and stay on target and in position for a count of one after-

ward. Release the trigger slowly until it resets, and you can begin a second shot as needed.

Now take those fundamentals and apply them with field-shooting positions. The basic and most accurate, of course, is prone. When using the prone position, it is important to get directly behind and in line with the rifle and not offset like the old green army men figures. This can be modified for special situations, such as use of cover, etc., but at the moment we are simply looking at marksmanship.

One very easy way to use prone with these rifles is to use the magazine monopod. Simply place the bottom of the magazine on the ground and line up behind the rifle, relaxing into the position. We have seen students take head shots with iron-sighted rifles at 200 yards using this method, so it is very workable and stable.

While prone is very stable and increases the potential for

If the shooter finds he needs more elevation of his knees, the careful placement of a magazine or two will solve the problem.

The positions and dynamics of CQB (Close Quarters Battle) shooting are different than what is necessary for intermediate-range marksmanship.

accuracy, in the field it may be a problem if undulating terrain or vegetation block your line of sight to the target. In such cases you may have to abandon prone for a higher-level position. Almost as stable a position is sitting. There are various types of sitting, so experiment to see which is most suitable for you and your body type, and any gear you may be using. The three basic ones are crossed-legged boots close, cross-legged boots far and open legged.

Again, the idea is to reduce the use of muscles to sustain the position and promote the use of bone. To do this, you might consider altering the position of your boots farther under the thighs to better support the legs and subsequently

the arms. One trick I learned in my travels overseas is to simply wedge a magazine between the boot and the leg to raise the platform to further reduce muscle stress. You can also use a tall rucksack or even an artificial vertical support.

Kneeling is another shooting position that can aid marksmanship. Not as stable as sitting or prone, it is far more stable than standing. The classic kneeling involves a 90-degree relationship between the legs, with the back of the arm rested atop the knee. This, of course, like the other positions, can be altered for field use to take advantage of terrain and cover, but it is best to learn the classic basic position first before doing so. The same

issues of tall rucksacks and vertical supports can be used with kneeling or its slightly lower and faster alternative, the squatting position.

Standing is the least stable and most challenging of the shooting positions. The classic marksmanship-based standing, or, as some call it, off-hand, is almost forgotten about by the tactical shooting crowd. The focus is so much on close-quarters battle and fighting at room distances that almost everyone teaches running the rifle like it were an MP5. That is fine for the close-range world, but not so workable for the longer distances. Yet this position may be needed if the intervening vegetation disqualifies any other rested position.

The marksmanship standing position is more bladed and less inclined forward than the CQB version. It also seeks to stabilize and control, rather than drive, the rifle. One is not better than the other. It simply depends on the environment you are fighting in. The support arm is held as close to vertical as possible, and the firing arm is held in a way as to maintain a shoulder pocket and a good cheekweld.

In the prone position, maintain cheekweld and bone support. Just make sure you don't get so relaxed that you lose focus.

If you find lower positions unsuitable due to an interrupted line of fire, using the sling with a vertical support will yield almost as accurate a shot as prone.

Correct placement in the shoulder and the establishment of a cheekweld are essential fundamentals. You will not shoot well without them.

While a standing position can be very accurate, it can be enhanced via the use of the sling and use of the sling and a vertical support if such is available. One can even use the services of a standing spotter's shoulder, as taught in sniper school (just be sure you use his right shoulder so the brass doesn't eject into his face).

These positions and fundamentals should be included in the daily dry work of any aspiring rifleman. With these skills and fundamentals, you will be able to take amazing shots. Without them, you will miss anything outside of 10 yards. The Kalashnikov platform, suitably arranged, can be amazingly accurate. As we delve more into the addition of modern optics, such as the ACOG, and the conversion to alternative calibers, such as the 6.5 Grendel, we will see the death and burial of the myth of the inaccurate AK. The technicians have done their part in that area, and now it is time for Kalashnikov trainers and shooters to be up to the rifles being built for them. Taking these suggestions to heart will give you a big head start in that area.

The term "sniper" has taken on a very lofty and elite meaning in America due in part to the "sniper media." But it can also be credited to the elitist attitude of many sniper schools and trainers. That same media promotes the idea that one needs to spend the equivalent of a couple of house payments on a rifle, an equal amount on the scope, then spend his free time memorizing ballistic charts and mil-dot measurements.

But stop to consider that many of history's best-known snipers did not have even the equal of a modern rack-grade hunting rifle.

What they did have was solid, reliable equipment; a solid understanding of marksmanship; and a hunter's heart. By today's perspectives, their education (or lack thereof), lowly equipment and humble standards would not even qualify them to enter the sniper's bar for a lukewarm beer.

The best perspective comes from a good friend of mine who is currently serving as a PSD contractor in Iraq. When we were discussing the sniper terminology on Warrior Talk (warriortalk.com), he posted a poll of sorts to the members. The question: If he

YOU CAN AFFORD TO BUILD A CAPABLE RIFLE TO ADDRESS MOST ENGAGEMENTS.

BY GABE SUAREZ

With a shorter barrel, fitted handguard and high-quality optic, even this Soviet-inspired rifle can deliver less than two-MOA performance.

were standing post in Iraq and a .30-caliber bullet narrowly missed his head, impacting on the brick wall behind him, what should he yell out to his teammates?

    A. Squad designated marksman!

    B. Precision long-range shooter!

    C. Military-trained and qualified sniper!

    D. Sniper!

Most readers agreed it would be the last option. Various discussions we have had with assigned, trained and qualified snipers from various militaries around the world, including U.S. special operations soldiers,

Russian Spetsnaz snipers and a couple of "Irregular Force" snipers from the Balkans War, reveal that while snipers do have the rare and occasional shot outside 500 yards, the vast majority of sniping has occurred well inside the 500-yard interval. The reason will become evident to anyone who grabs a rifle and a ruck, leaves the known-distance marksmanship worship center and ventures out into the woods. You cannot see people much farther away than about 400 yards.

Moreover, when we get away from the aspect of scoring targets and focus more on eliminating targets, we realize that we don't need to hit the X-ring on the human adversary and that torso hits will accomplish the task. If we look at a human adversary's target zone, or his torso, we see that it is roughly 18x24 inches. A rifle that can deliver three MOA can easily perform this job, and many rack-grade AKs will deliver three MOA.

As a benchmark, I think the ability to place head shots out to 200 yards and body shots out to 500 yards is good for any sniper rifle, and it's what we will set as a reasonable and reachable goal. That roughly translates as a six-inch group at 200 yards and a 15-inch group at 500 yards. A three-MOA rifle is well in the running.

A full-length PSL easily handles steel at 500 yards.

This Saiga 308 delivered two MOA, making it well capable of fulfilling the mission discussed.

While we have seen the rise of the Tabuk rifle in Iraq, it is not what we are looking for here. The Tabuk is essentially a repurposed RPK with an optic on it. In class we have seen good shots with such rifles reach out to 800 yards, but they are limited by the caliber. The 7.62x39mm is a great intermediate rifle cartridge, but it lacks the qualities of a good sniper cartridge such as the 7.62x54R or 7.62x51 NATO. Those qualities include the ability to reach for distance with authority, hit solidly out there, resist wind and other atmospheric conditions and be relatively unaffected by intervening brush. Those are all things that the 7.62x39, 5.45x39 and 5.56x45, for that matter, cannot deliver as well as the 7.62x54R or 7.62x51. Moreover, those two cali-

bers are easily available today. The 7.62x51 is available in a multitude of flavors from high-dollar custom match-quality rounds to delinked machine-gun ammo in rusty boxes. The 7.62x54R does not have quite the variety, but it makes up for it in economy. It is the lowest-priced centerfire .30-caliber ammo you can find.

Rifles that would be considered for the Kalashnikov sniper must include the SVD, the Saiga 308 and the PSL in 7.62x54R. While I have fired SVDs both in the U.S. and overseas, they are extremely rare here in the U.S. and discussing them would be akin to an article entitled "What Cannot Be Obtained." We will confine the study to the Saiga 308

The Saiga 308 rifle, suitably modified back into its combat form, performs beautifully in the sniper role.

The PSL rifle benefits from the use of good ammunition, a high-quality scope and a bipod.

The Saiga 308 served as the platform for this rifle by Red Jacket Firearms.

and the PSL, which are both available to the American shooter.

SAIGA 308

The Saiga 308 can be had in 16- or 21-inch barrel length. One may be tempted to get the longer barrel, but I think for the distances that this rifle is intended for, a 16-inch pipe would be a better choice. As a point of fact, at a recent Guerrilla Sniper class put on at Suarez International, my firearms training academy, we had a 16-inch-barreled Saiga 308 with Federal Match ammo hitting steel at 1,000 yards.

The rifle needs to be desporterized. One reason, of course, is the aesthetics, and another reason is for handling purposes. Pistol-grip conversions are not only easier to shoot well, they allow you to get rid of the strange and spongy trigger the imported configuration has issued. Also, the rifle needs a flash hider.

This particular Saiga 308 was worked on by Will Hayden at Red Jacket Firearms in Baton Rouge, Louisiana (redjacket-firearms.com). The barrel was cut to 16 inches, and a flash hider and modified front sight base were added. We also put on an Ultimak handguard, mostly to add a bipod, but we learned later that it also improved accuracy.

A VEPR scope mount and Burris 3-9X BallisticPlex scope gave us a solid mount for our optics and a BDC out to 500 yards. On the Saiga and the PSL we opted for an American scope rather than the typical POSP Com-Bloc optics found on these rifles. The reason was simple. We found we needed more eye relief than those scopes provided. The trigger was replaced with a Red Star Arms kit (which should be mandatory for all AKs intended for precision work). We removed the buttstock and added a Vltor stock extension and a Magpul stock to allow for an adjustable LOP, which we realized was helpful with this rifle.

The rifle is handicapped by a lack of good magazines. The magazines issued with it have an eight-round capacity. They can be modified by the end user to a 10-round configuration and be quite reliable that way, but it would be beneficial if higher-capacity, military-grade magazines were available for it.

A rifle is only as good as the ammo it is fed. Often when we hear discussions about the in-accuracy of the Kalashnikov system, we find that the ammo used was the cheapest surplus stuff one could find buried in some Cold War bunker. Good ammo will make all the difference. This rifle, with Prvi Partisan 168-grain Match, yielded 1 1/2 MOA at 100 yards, well within our requirements.

Shooting with field-expedient supports, as found in many urban areas, is easy with light rifles like Kalashnikov-based sniper platforms.

When an artificial rest is unavailable, snipers can enlist the use of their spotters, as this Saiga sniper does in the Guerrilla Sniper Course at Suarez International.

PSL

The next rifle is the PSL. The PSL (Puşcă Semiautomată cu Lunetă, or "scoped semi-automatic rifle") is a Romanian military marksman rifle. It has also been called the PSL-54c, Romak III, FPK, FPK Dragunov and SSG-97 and was sold in various configurations.

The PSL as it comes from the factory is ready to go, but it can be improved considerably by a good Kalashnikov 'smith. This one was a project given to Jim Fuller at Rifle Dynamics in Las Vegas, Nevada. First order of business was replacing the stock trigger with the Red Star Arms kit (redstararms. com). This rifle now has a trigger more at

home on a Remington 700 PSS than a Romanian PSL. I had the same eye relief, LOP issues, so we discarded the original surplus scope as well as the factory stock.

We used a Romanian PSL 54c stock from Rhineland Arms (troupsystems.com). It has a number of stock configurations for this rifle. This particular stock is made of solid American walnut and includes an adjustable cheekrest, rubber recoil pad and contoured forearm. The cheekrest is made of a medium hard rubber, as is the recoil pad, to reduce felt recoil. The forearm has two threaded inserts for a sling swivel or bipod mounting. The stock is longer, for a length of pull increased to 151/4, and it can be reduced

The Romanian PSL serves as a fine starting point for a light and compact precision rifle.

to 14 inches by cutting the wood. It came unfinished, but the technical services staff at Suarez International was able to apply a decent oil finish.

Jim Fuller also cut the barrel from its long 24 inches to a light and handy 19 inches. This not only makes the rifle handier, it adds to barrel stiffness, which increases accuracy. When we run the rifle with a suppressor, we see far less group drift with the shorter barrels. We added a custom PKM-style flash hider that is both short and effective.

For the optics system, I settled on the following. For the mount we used the Belarus low-mount BP-02A. It comes with a Picatinny rail to mount any optic the user desires. The BP02 was a gift from one of our friends in the former Soviet nation, but they can be easily found in the U.S. for either the AK-47 rail or the SVD Dragunov rifle and Romanian Romak 3/SSG-97. I used a set of low Warne QD rings we had in the armory at our facility.

The scope was an easy choice. I chose the Leatherwood Hi-Lux 1-4X CMR (Close Medium Range) scope. While we may eventually consider something with a little more magnification, this scope was highly recommended by both Marco Vorobiev and David Fortier, and in my testing it lives up to their recommendations. The relatively short 30mm tube scope does not add much weight to the PSL. The 30mm tube also lets in a lot of light for a bright and visible target image.

The circular reticle is reminiscent of the Leupold MR/T and helps in quick target acquisition. The lower crosshair in the reticle features a BDC calibrated for standard .223 and .308 service ammo out to 600 meters. The ballistics of the 7.62x54R is close enough to the .308 that the BDC worked fine for our purposes. The center dot and the small circle of the reticle are illuminated in a bright and visible green for utility in reduced lighting conditions.

This rifle, with Wolf Gold Medal 168-grain Match and Czech Silvertip, yielded two MOA and 2½ MOA at 100 yards, respectively. This was well within our requirements as well.

BEYOND THE RIFLE

One important point to those who have desired adding a sniper rifle to their armory but have been held back by the high price of a Knights Armament SR25 or Accuracy International rifle: Either of these rifles can be had ready to go, as described, with a good U.S.-made optic for little more than $1,500. And with a few additions, either of these rifles will allow a shooter who understands marksmanship to hit anything he wants at the distances where most sniping actually takes place. With the money saved, the end user could invest in a training class or two and a bunker full of practice ammo to develop and maintain his sniper skills.

SNUBNOSE
KALASHNIKOV

CAN THE AK FILL THE ROLL OF A PDW?   BY GABE SUAREZ

Kalashnikov's PDW variant is frequently (and incorrectly) referred to as a Krinkov, in the same way that Germany's MP-38 was usually called a Schmeisser.

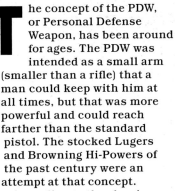

The concept of the PDW, or Personal Defense Weapon, has been around for ages. The PDW was intended as a small arm (smaller than a rifle) that a man could keep with him at all times, but that was more powerful and could reach farther than the standard pistol. The stocked Lugers and Browning Hi-Powers of the past century were an attempt at that concept.

According to the classic definition, a personal defense weapon is a compact semi-automatic or fully automatic firearm similar in size to a submachine gun, but firing an armor-piercing round (often proprietary), which gives it better range, accuracy and penetrating capability than a submachine gun firing pistol-caliber cartridges.

Sometime after World War II, the PDW idea seemed to drop out of favor, possibly because of the proliferation of the submachine gun. Still, while the pistol-caliber-chambered SMG has some interesting capabilities, it also has some tactical liabilities. Primarily, the proliferation of body armor

in recent years, coupled with a focus on urban combat, has made submachine guns ineffective at some missions.

The PDW concept was reborn some years ago in the form of the HK MP7, a PDW version of HK's ubiquitous MP5. This was basically an MP5K with a buttstock, and it was originally intended for air and vehicle crews.

Among other reasons, the PDW concept has not been widely successful because PDWs are not significantly cheaper to manufacture than full-size infantry rifles. They are also more expensive than most SMGs, while being less effective in scenarios where armor-piercing ammunition is unavailable or unnecessary (such as most civilian and law enforcement applications).

Moreover, the potential military market for PDWs has been diminished due to the introduction of mini-carbines based on full-size assault rifles (such as the M4 Carbine variant of the M16A2) that retain most of the features of and compatibility with their full-size relatives. Additionally, PDWs classically, and quite

PDWs cost about the same as a full-size rifle, but are a lot more handy.

often, require a special cartridge, such as the 5.7x28mm cartridge for the FN P90 or the 4.6x30mm for the HK MP7, which are not compatible with either existing pistol or rifle rounds. The quartermaster's job being what it is, the complexity of a special round for a special weapon often dooms a concept.

The PDW class as it exists today evolved into a hybrid of a submachine gun and a carbine, retaining the compact size and ammunition capacity of the former while adding the ammunition power, accuracy and penetration of the latter.

Though they never became very popular for military applications, many personal defense weapons have found their way into the hands of special security details and some special forces as direct replacements for the larger and difficult-to-conceal submachine guns.

According to the definition and concept, I think the perfect PDW is the short-barreled AKSU, alternatively known as a Krinkov or, more correctly, the Suchka. Let's look at the classic definition and requirements to see if the short AK fits the bill.

A PDW must be as small as an SMG. Immediately, this requires a short barrel and, unless one is an official agency, incurs the accompanying SBR licensing issues. So we begin the exercise with the clear assumption we will need to deal with the entire NFA registration process from the beginning. Many people are intimidated by the

This equipment would be familiar to any Soviet veteran of the Afghan war.

Form 1 or Class 3 process, but having gone through it a few times now, I can say it is far easier than obtaining a concealed carry permit. It is not a difficult thing at all and certainly nothing to be afraid of. I encourage anyone who lives in a state that allows it to take advantage of it.

The PDW can be semiauto or selective fire. From our perspective, and purely for economic reasons, it must be semiauto. It's not that we can't locate any full-auto versions in the U.S., but they are costly. Don't dismiss the concept because it is semiauto. We have run experiments with our semiauto firearms. We have had our staff shoot the full-auto qualification courses of

An Airsoft competitor in full competition rig.

various agencies and special units (with both assault rifles and semiauto submachine guns) and found we did not lose anything by using a semiauto.

Moreover, I have discussed the matter with several former European and Israeli operators with a considerable amount of combat experience who were equipped with both the HK MP5 and UZI, and none of them can ever recall an operational use of his PDW in anything but a semiauto mode.

The PDW must be capable of penetrating armor and other mediums. Agreed. I think that any shoulder-fired rifle, carbine or PDW should have this capability because adversaries rarely stand still like a target on the range. They move and use cover. And even back in the 1990s when I was operational, they all seemed to wear body armor. So the ability to breach that cover and penetrate that vest is essential.

There are various ways to do this. I am dubious of the new micro-calibers. While the term "armor piercing" has caused terror and night sweats in most of the civilian gun community, let's face it: Even a cheap box of .30-30 Win. hunting ammo will do what is needed here. It is even better if the weapon is chambered in 7.62x39mm, which outpenetrates most of the widely seen rifle cartridges available today.

So the simple solution: A Suchka (known to the uninformed as a Krinkov) easily

accomplishes the requirements for the Kalashnikov PDW. To test my theory, I bought an Arsenal SLR-107 UR in 7.62x39mm. This is the long-barreled rifle with the body of an AKSU-74 and the stock of an AK-100. We submitted paperwork to the ATF in December 2008 and got it back in early May 2009. The entire licensing process took a total wait of five months—a long wait perhaps, but at a time when you could not even find ammo, I understand.

Why did I select the 7.62x39 over the 5.56 NATO? Because while the 5.56 may be more lethal on paper and within a close-range envelope, my studies and discussions with the current U.S. military veterans, as well as former operators from the Soviet Union and other areas of the world, have shown me that the 5.56x45mm is not immediately incapacitating. This is especially the case if it needs to penetrate any intermediate barriers first. And, of course, the 5.56x45 NATO does not penetrate intermediate mediums as well as alternative calibers such as the 7.62x39mm.

The 7.62x39mm may not be as ultimately lethal or ballistically refined as the 5.56, but it is far more immediately incapacitating. Moreover, the .30-caliber bullet will penetrate just about everything much better. Yes, a 6.8 SPC AK would be nice, but at the time of this discussion no such animal exists.

Once the NFA paperwork returned, we took off the long part of the barrel in a sort of lathe-driven circumcision. We were left with a very short 8½-inch barrel that was flush with the front sight/gas chamber assembly. We added the Bulgarian Four Piece Flash Hider. The dwell time on this

By definition, a PDW must have the ballistic effectiveness to defeat soft body armor. Pistol-caliber submachine guns just aren't up to the task.

rifle is very short, since the muzzle is nearly right on top of the gas chamber. The Russians developed several units to increase reliability by increasing pressure. The Bulgarian Four Piece Flash Hider is one of these. This unit acts to increase back pressure, sending gas back into the action, making a reliable rifle even more so. Results were a very short and packable Suchka PDW—semiauto, small as an HK MP5 SMG and capable of penetrating anything any adversary would wish to hide behind or wear short of armored steel. Think of a .30-caliber, high-capacity, six-pound MP5 and you will get a good idea of what this is about.

It is no more expensive than anything worthwhile today. I paid the princely sum of $1,200 in November 2008 (in our new and improved—changed—America, it might cost a little more, and the government's fee added $200). Try to find an MP5 PDW, an FN or anything like this for less than $2,000. Good luck.

One other comment in the PDW literature mentions that they are "effective in scenarios where armor-piercing capability is not needed." This one is touchy. You certainly don't think a .30-caliber pill flying at 2,000 fps will stay inside of anything, but then again, that needs to be tested. The results will be affected greatly by ammunition choices.

Ammunition choices could affect this in various ways. For example, Cor-Bon has recently brought out a 7.62x39mm load in its DPX line. This is the ammo that normally rides in my magazines. The Cor-Bon DPX launches a 123-grain Barnes X solid-copper bullet at 2,300 fps. When the bullet hits an adversary, it expands to create a large wound channel, yet the bullet base remains solid and intact for greater retained weight and penetration.

Another interesting ammunition choice is Cor-Bon's Hunter Line, listing a 108-grain Multi-Purpose Green bullet at 2,500 fps. This hunting bullet was originally developed for military and law enforcement applications. MPG bullets feature a highly frangible, powdered-metal, copper-tin core inside a gilding metal jacket.

Unlike frangible bullets lacking a protective jacket, MPG bullets remain intact under the rigors of handling, feeding and firing. This round shows great promise as a limited-penetration round for the 7.62x39mm in CQB.

Out of a short barrel like this, velocities will range in the area of 1,800 to 2,000 fps, depending on the loading—not magnum performance nor as refined as many modern cartridges, but I doubt any detractors of the Kalashnikov system would want to stand in front of a Suchka loaded with 30 rounds of Cor-Bon DPX inside 100 yards.

I have run the AK PDW now for several months, teaching several classes with it and taking it along with me on weekly back-country training runs. The rifle is handy and easy to carry. It is fast into action.

Owing to its short length and lighter weight, it is much faster up to the shoulder—or on the move, in fact—than a standard-length Kalashnikov. While it is intended for close-quarters battle applications and not really for long-range shooting, we found it quite easy to hit our steel silhouettes at 200 meters.

This PDW would profit greatly from a red dot sight like an Aimpoint Micro. At the time of this writing I have been told that Ultimak is considering manufacturing one of its excellent gas tube rails for the Arsenal SLR series of Suchka. That rail setup, with an Aimpoint Micro (and the ability to add a removable flashlight setup), will make this little blaster into a very flexible package capable of use in extreme CQB environments as well as reaching into the full-size tactical rifle category. It is a good time to be a Kalashnikov shooter.

Gabe Suarez is the CEO of Suarez International USA. His company has been conducting training in the Kalashnikov system all over the world since 2005. His websites are www.suarezinternational.com and www.warriortalk.com.

While a PDW might not be the choice for precision shooting, it's accurate and powerful enough for most law enforcement situations.

A VIEW FROM THE OTHER SIDE

INTRODUCING REALITY INTO FIREARMS TRAINING

BY MARCO VOROBIEV

At Behind Lines, sniper/DMR courses based on Soviet doctrine are bread and butter, but other courses are offered.

I have always had a fascination with firearms. So it was only natural that after moving to the United States I absorbed the American gun culture, or maybe it absorbed me. As a kid growing up in the Soviet Union, one is exposed to guns at an early age. First it's a trip to the market and air rifle range with your dad. Then in fifth through eighth grade, there is a field trip to the DOSAAF (Volunteers Society to Assist Army, Air Force and Navy) range for .22-caliber rifle exercises. This is mandatory for boys (Future Conscripts) and optional for girls, though there was nearly 100 percent attendance by both sexes every time.

It was not uncommon for a middle school to have a .22 rifle range in its basement where students would exercise their skills at least twice a year. At the same time, numerous sport clubs offered a variety of shooting disciplines, from competitive pistol to trap and skeet, each available to any kid. Then came ninth and tenth grades with the twice-per-week Beginners Military Preparation Course.

And that is the path I took to the wonderful world of Kalashnikov rifles. Apart from the usual military-type drilling—

A variety of target types are used during training, including Soviet-pattern targets.

marching in formation, digging fox holes, putting on a gas mask and such—the goal of the Beginners Military Preparation class was to make you proficient with an AK. As a final exam, you had to complete two exercises: the field tactical exercise and a trip to a real military range. At the range you were given an AK (the real full-auto military rifle) and told to shoot three rounds on semi-auto into 100-meter static targets and six rounds on full auto at resetting metal silhouette targets set at 200- to 400-meter ranges. Just think, by age 16 all Soviet boys and most Soviet girls had fired a fully automatic AK and could fieldstrip it with their eyes closed.

Then came a draft into the Soviet armed forces and two years of mandatory service. As fate would have it, I wound up in the Spetsnaz Training Center in Chirchik, Uzbekistan (then part of the Soviet Union), for preparation for deployment to Afghanistan. There I served for 16 months, first as a sniper within a fire-support group and later as a rifleman in an assault unit. I had a chance to carry both the sexiest rifle in existence (which, in my humble opinion, is the SVD), as well as one that was more of a garden-variety workhorse, the AKS-74.

In Chirchik I reported to the 467 Spetsnaz Training

Marco Vorobiev is the founder of the Behind Lines facility. A Spetsnaz sniper who served in Afghanistan, his training is intended to be very practical.

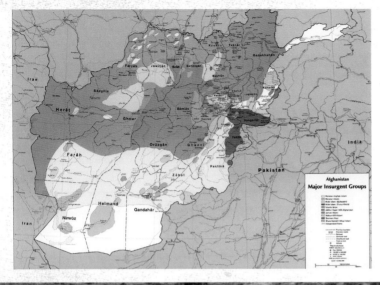

Afghanistan
Major Insurgent Groups

While engaging students, the instructor passes on the information that he learned with his own sweat.

The sniper/DMR classes are not limited to Com Bloc rifles. Here Hensoldt's importer, Nathan Hunt, takes a shot with his AI from the back of an M35A2 truck.

Regiment. Since "training" was in its name, training is what we did. We were training for war.

Three months to the date after first putting on a uniform, I was ready, or deemed ready by the Soviet army, and able to kill and be killed for the Motherland.

If I look back and ask myself whether we were properly trained, I'd say that at the time of departure for Afghanistan we were prepared and ready for anything. When we arrived and joined our respective units, I realized just how little I knew and how much more I needed to learn. My Afghan stint turned into a long and hazardous training session.

One cannot help but marvel at the training opportunities that are available to shooting enthusiasts in America. Not only can the individual lawfully possess a gun, he can take numerous courses that will train him in anything from shooting techniques to proper maintenance for that firearm.

The most popular courses these days appear to be the ones that offer training involving the "black" guns or military-style rifles, such as the M4s and AKs. Great! If you have them, use them, I always say. But what's available? The majority of courses today concentrate on specific gun applications within CQC situations, military or police-type training in a boxed-in environment shooting at static targets and sweeping through plywood mazes.

A group of NCOs and enlisted soldiers from the 5/4 CAV came down for a standard carbine class, then came back for a foreign weapons class. Behind Lines does its best to cater to the specific needs of the military.

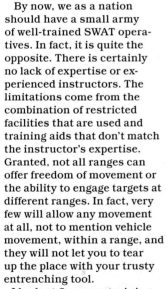

Low-light and night fires are an important part of training that are often ignored by shooting schools.

By now, we as a nation should have a small army of well-trained SWAT operatives. In fact, it is quite the opposite. There is certainly no lack of expertise or experienced instructors. The limitations come from the combination of restricted facilities that are used and training aids that don't match the instructor's expertise. Granted, not all ranges can offer freedom of movement or the ability to engage targets at different ranges. In fact, very few will allow any movement at all, not to mention vehicle movement, within a range, and they will not let you to tear up the place with your trusty entrenching tool.

I look at firearms training as more of a comprehensive exercise that should include a variety of infantry preparation elements, not just proper body position, breathing and trigger pull. Setting up your shooting position, operating within a unit, following mission-specific

orders, managing your load, the proper use of your kit, concealment, movement, vehicle mount and dismount, your responsibilities within a unit and other must-know information are not generally offered by regular training courses, as few have the expertise or ability to offer this curriculum.

If you look at the military-type firearm that most training courses are built around, it was designed as an instrument of war and deployed as such.

When considering training with such a firearm, one should look at a much broader picture. The gun is just a tool, and if applied correctly, it will help you achieve an overall objective.

That is why when our Spetsnaz unit prepared for a mission, the number and types of rifles and other assets were determined first. That is how the unit's strength was assessed. Unlike regular Soviet Motorized Infantry units where everyone had

Here the author explains the next drill to his class. Soviet methods and thinking are often very different than the norm in the West.

Man-on-man drills push students to new levels. Here a soldier from the 1st ID sprints to a barricade to engage simulated threats.

a specific profession with proper training, Spetsnaz was cross training its troops. The infantry APC driver-mechanic was just that—a driver and mechanic—and the radio operator was first and foremost a radio operator. Of course, they could handle their issued rifles, but anything past that was questionable. Spetsnaz soldiers were cross trained on all small arms and equipment that were utilized by the unit, including hardware such as APCs, grenade launchers, large-caliber rifles, night vision and radios.

The idea is to use a firearm in the broader sense, along with the kit, and with a broader purpose. It should be seen merely as a tool in your versatile tool box.

Enter the specialized training facility Behind Lines, where this gap in knowledge is filled by introducing several reality-based elements to make training more comprehensive. Having a unique set of tools available to us at Behind Lines, in Chapman, KS, makes it easy for us to conduct unconventional and interesting courses. Every class includes movement within a unit or in pairs through vast land, providing an opportunity for scouting drills; two "deuce and a half" army trucks to simulate vehicle-borne deployment and counterambush; a rifle range offering challenging shots at zero to 800 yards from several positions, as well as direct-report range targets;

and wooded areas and grassy hills that allow concealment and ambush training.

Recently introduced as part of every class is a night-fire exercise, which provides trainees with a unique opportunity to gain an understanding of night shooting and night-vision equipment. Students who have their own NV equipment are encouraged to bring it. Behind Lines also offers several Soviet-type small arms equipped with NV, including the rarest SVDS sniper rifle.

Obviously, having a combat veteran teach a class is a great help, bringing the element of reality into training. While engaging students, the instructor passes on the morsels of information that he earned with his own sweat.

Furthermore, these classes include instructions right out of Soviet army manuals. The Soviet way of doing things is different from what the average student is exposed to here in the States. Some of methods are so successful that today they are being employed by the U.S. military in Afghanistan. Behind Lines classes provide an opportunity for trainees to get a glimpse of how the "other guys" did it.

Behind Lines offers a variety of training. Some of the exotic "toys" that are available to trainees include this fully automatic PKM machine gun.

Though this type of training exposes students to realistic elements of military training, the classes attract students from all walks of life such as long-range rifle shooters, history buffs, serious collectors (including myself) who want to know how their stuff works, government contractors and active military personnel who are awaiting deployment.

Understandably, it is impossible to learn in two or three days what is most effectively taught over months or even years. However, it is possible to acquire a new skill or two in such a short time and further develop that skill by practicing.

All in all, the type of training conducted at Behind Lines offers a unique and comprehensive experience. My view of training—any training—is that it must have a goal or objective. As with continuing education, we strive to learn more so that we can advance by implementing what we've learned. Firearms training is no different.

Pick a subject you most want to master, and go for it. At the very least you'll have a fun weekend, and you may learn something new.

SOURCE

Behind Lines
734-477-0700
www.behindlines.net

As Behind Lines is located next to Fort Riley, soldiers from the 1st ID are often in attendance. Here a group of students from the 5/4 CAV pose after finishing instruction prior to their deployment to Iraq.

COLD WINTER TRAINING AT
BEHIND LINES

LEARN TO PREPARE YOUR RIFLE AND KIT FOR THE CHILLY EXTREME.

BY MARCO VOROBIEV

Weather has a profound effect on us and everything around us. And nothing affects us more than cold. The military is no exception. Cold weather affects the military more than civilians. The military has to fight wars and defend nations in it, and so it must retain its capabilities whatever the conditions.

The military's readiness and ability to operate in adverse conditions often determine the outcome of a battle and possibly the entire campaign. Just remember Napoleon's Russia campaign in 1812 and, some 130 years later, Hitler's Operation Barbarossa in 1941. Many Western historians like to credit General Winter with the Russian victories, as if Russian soldiers weren't involved and the French and Germans, after getting frostbitten and becoming hypothermic, decided to turn around and go home of their own accord. On the contrary, it was the Russian armed forces that sent them packing. Suffering through the same frigid conditions, they managed to deliver a defeat to their enemy. This is when training, gear, equipment, weapons and the ability to use those weapons come into play and dictate which side comes out victorious.

Weather can destroy even the most carefully prepared plans. You have to prepare for it and train for it. I did.

During my 16-month stint as a Spetsnaz trooper, I lived and fought through two Afghan winters in the rugged Hindu Kush Mountains of Badakhshan.

I grew up in the foothills of the Southern Ural Mountains, so the prospect of going south did not seem bad as far as weather was concerned. Boy, was I wrong. Never in my life have I seen so much snow and felt as cold as I did in Afghanistan.

War in Afghanistan in the winter takes on different characteristics, depending on where you are. The Muj activities in the north would decrease, resulting in a lesser number of ambushes on our supply convoys. Most of the rebels' efforts were concentrated on rebuilding their units' strength and stronghold fortifications. The considerable snowfall in the mountains blocks numerous passages, hindering the movements of Muj resupply caravans.

A sudden increase in the male population in local villages is a good sign that it's just too damn cold for insurgents in the mountains; they come down for well-deserved R&R. While the Afghan police, security service and Afghan National Army kept busy in the winter months by hunting rebels

in towns and villages, we would switch from our regular ambush activities to more addressed raids. We took the fight to our enemy by raiding their strongholds; destroying their weapons, ammunition and medicine caches; and blocking and hitting their units in the villages.

But to tell you that my unit was an "all weather" unit would be a blatant lie. Sometimes the conditions were so bad that air-support aircraft could not take off, thus making any raid with helo insertion and/or extraction and support impossible. In situations like that, armor would be used for insertions, extractions, and fire and tactical support, along with the closest firebase, but again within reason. In the mountains, snowfall means avalanches, resulting in blocked roads and lost lives. Because we had to operate in these conditions that were less than hospitable, we trained. We trained not only in how to use our weapons, but also on how to use our gear.

The hardest thing for me to get used to was the temperature fluctuation from day to night. If you did not anticipate it, you were in trouble, and several Soviet units learned the hard way. Most of our issued cold-weather clothing was quilted and insulated with cotton. Regardless of how warm it was, that cotton insulation made it ridiculously heavy to wear and cumbersome to move in. So we

took the gear that was made available for us and, through trial and error, made it work because we had to be proficient with our weapons and our gear in any environment.

Winter doesn't add only discomfort, it also adds weight to your kit and changes the geometry of movement and shooting. It takes what you've learned as a soldier and tosses it out the window. And that is what gave me the idea to offer a winter tactical/firearm course at our school Behind Lines (behindlines.net). Two classes were designed around Soviet Spetsnaz tactics employed in Afghanistan in the 1980s during the Soviet Afghan campaign.

We held our Cold Weather/Winter Spetsnaz Sniper Class in late January. Instead of our usual base of operation in Chapman, Kansas, we were able to secure a range at Sayre Sportsmens Club in Athens, Pennsylvania, that offered ranges from zero to 500 meters, wooded and clear areas for field exercises and a heated clubhouse for classroom time.

The weather decided to cooperate for the duration of the class. Temperatures hovered around 20 degrees during the day and dropped to the low teens at night. Snow came down for a day and a half and was very heavy at times. Needless to say, the conditions were perfect for a challenging cold-weather class.

The students who made up this class were about the same as those attending any other of our regular courses—which is to say, they came from all walks of life: a former tank commander, a former army reserve officer, an active member of the Texas National Guard and shooting enthusiasts. All but one had some long-range rifle experience.

For their guns, we saw the usual rifle salad: a couple of .308-chambered AR-10s, one Bravo Company DMR rifle in .223, an SVD and a couple of Romanian PSLs, one of which was provided by Century International Arms.

Students had been instructed on what to bring, which included warm clothing, proper footwear, hats, gloves, load-bearing gear and snow camo. The majority of students had various models of surplus Gore-Tex outer-shell clothing, one had a standard-issue Russian enlisted winter uniform and one student sported his civilian cold-weather gear. Half the class had LB vests that they had used for other courses; the rest had to improvise with standard surplus belt pouches, coat pockets and backpacks. All but one brought some kind of snow camouflage. Three students opted for ponchos, two had standard Russian/Soviet winter camo oversuits and one wound up using a white bed sheet as a cape—simple, but effective.

I wore my standard Soviet-issue mountain uniform, which kept me very comfortable throughout the class. However, in reserve I had several options, ranging from a Russian cotton quilted winter set to modern Primaloft-insulated Otte Gear HP Parka and Softie-insulated ProForce Equipment (Snugpak) Sleeka coat and pants.

After a classroom session and safety briefing, instructors helped a couple of students with their gear, adjusting straps on clothing, instructing them on load distribution and helping with snow camo. Then we headed out to the range.

At the range everybody had to reestablish his zero at 100 meters. Two things adversely affected the original sighting of all guns. First, the lower-than-normal temperatures caused rapid cooling, affecting the dynamics of the guns' barrels. Second, the comfort level of lying prone in the snow with extra-thick clothing affected aim angles. Almost all students experienced minor to major deviations from their original zeros. However, the cold weather had a positive affect on PSL rifles. After zeroing, we moved into rapid-fire drills. This is when the PSL usually starts to drop POI due to the barrel overheating. This time, no matter how long the series, all shots stayed in one general location. Another inherent PSL feature that became a clear advantage was the rifle's short stock. It worked well with the extra padding of thick winter clothing. However, a proper cheek-weld was still to be desired.

Plain white snow camouflage is one the most effective patterns for snowy environments.

After several series of rapid-fire exercises, students moved to timed multiple target drills in line with the principle "multiple shots, multiple kills." Everyone had to engage several targets across the entire field. This is where students stepped out of their comfort zone, which was clearly evident. Once they deviated from their natural angle of aim, the groups on several same shooter targets opened up significantly. We ran several drills with shooters engaging targets in patterns to get accustomed to rapid target acquisition. Another skill the students acquired during the first set was to double-tap every target—not in the sense of a carbine double-tapping technique, but rather a corrected follow-up shot in case the target moved.

At the end of the 100-meter, multiple-target drills, we broke for a lunch of buckwheat and pork, Soviet army-style, cooked over an open fire.

The second part of day one saw students moving into the fieldcraft portion of the course. They were introduced to unit movement, basic concealment techniques, how to build and conceal a shooting position and how little it takes to blend in and become totally invisible from distances as close as 25 yards. I still say that snow camo is the best pattern of camouflage, and a solid-white snow camo suit is the best because it mimics the light reflection of snow and allows you to conceal yourself even in the open field. Any dark spots and splotches will give away even the slightest movement. However, both patterns work well within brush or wooded areas.

Though the reflective properties of snow make it a great environment to blend in, it can also give you away just as easily. Foot tracks or any other disturbances will betray unit presence. Students were instructed in walking "in step" to hide the unit's strength and in approaching their positions from the rear so as not to disturb the front of their shooting nests.

When positions were set up, everyone drew range cards and started to range. The direct-report Action Target silhouettes and Alexander Arms reactive targets were set up at ranges of 150 to 350 meters. After proper ranging was completed, students gradually engaged targets and worked their way from closest to farthest, using reticle holdovers rather than the scopes' BDC turrets. We ran this drill several times, letting students get comfortable with using optics when engaging multiple targets through the depth on the entire field. When everyone had scored solid hits on targets at various ranges and memorized their holdovers, each student was given specific orders when targets in his card were called at random. As we anticipated, students were getting confident with their rifles and optics. Day one was done. It was time to draw first conclusions for what had worked and what hadn't.

All the guns worked well, even after their muzzles were dipped repeatedly into snow. All fed well,

except one PSL rifle with substandard magazines. This was easily corrected for day two by setting the faulty mags aside. All rifles functioned well in spite of loaded mags constantly getting dropped in the snow and then inserted into the gun. This happened throughout the class—even after the students were instructed to change their usual magazine handling and to prevent magazines and ammo from falling into the snow.

The biggest eye-opener for the students was their optics. They were instructed on how to protect their scopes' lenses from snow packing into objectives. This causes lenses to fog up, and if the snow is not removed it would melt and possibly penetrate sealed scopes, rendering optics useless. Several students still managed to drop their rifles into snow and then tried to blow the snow from the lenses instead of wiping it off, amplifying the fogging problem.

Most of the gear held up well. Almost everyone kept their bodies and appendages warm and dry. Three individuals (two students and one staff) soaked their boots. The students made the mistake of bringing summer boots; their boots got wet almost immediately and offered limited protection to their owners through the first day of

Students were put through a series of multi-target drills and got their first taste of lying in snow at a 100-meter firing line.

class. This was remedied by using plastic shopping bags to wrap them the next day. Military-model waterproof boots are better suited for what we do in the class. I wore standard-issue Soviet Paratrooper leather jump boots (smeared with Bear Grease ahead of time) over long cotton inner and long and thick wool outer socks. I felt no discomfort of any kind during the class. Lessons learned. Two things are your worst enemy in the winter environment: exposure and moisture.

Day two started much smoother. After a daylong learning session the day before, all students had their gear and rifles sorted out. Although Spetsnaz in Afghanistan was constantly springing ambushes on Muj resupply routes, there was always a chance of being ambushed by the insurgents as well. So we made ambush countermeasure drills a part of our Spetsnaz Sniper Class. Ambush is a surprising and very dynamic event, and readiness for it must be exercised. During an enemy ambush, the proper organization and application of fire in the ensuing firefight often determines an outcome. Concentrated fire by the entire unit on the enemy positions, striking or pinning their personnel, is an important measure that provides time for the unit to reorganize, move out of the kill zone and, possibly, mount a counter-maneuver.

First, we simulated an ambush on a foot patrol. Students working in teams of three had to engage multiple targets on the fly from unprepared positions. The drills included engaging a target, changing position and reengaging other targets as well as transitioning to a secondary weapon. Every student shot well after he got over the initial excitement. The problem that plagued most of them was snow clogging scopes and the open sights of the secondary weapon. Their accuracy went up significantly after deficiencies were pointed out and more attention was paid to weapon handling.

Next, the class entered a vehicle drills phase. There were several deployment exercises from stationary and moving vehicles. The latter exercise was used extensively in Afghanistan by the Spetsnaz to throw off enemy observers. At a turn in the road, the vehicle would slow down, at which time the troopers would roll off it and take cover before regrouping and continuing on their mission.

After lunch we continued with counter-ambush exercises. This time drills simulated an enemy ambush on a motorized convoy. Students had to engage targets from a moving vehicle. The first drill saw students in pairs firing at two Action Target humanoid steel silhouettes at 100 meters while moving in the truck in a lateral plane in relation to the targets. The students delivered an amazing 20 to 30 percent hit rate. The hit rate increased dramatically as the participants started getting used to holding on targets and timely trigger pulls. We switched to closer-contact engagement drills where the truck would drive students to and from several

Students practice ambush counter-measure drills included engaging targets from a moving vehicle.

plywood silhouette targets with the objective of engaging targets closest to farthest. This exercise was developed to counter the insurgents' suicidal grenade or handheld IED attacks; that is when during a firefight an element of enemy personnel would close on a vehicle in an attempt to throw an explosive device into an APC hatch or truck bed. Once again, as challenging as it was, the students achieved around a 30 to 40 percent hit rate.

Firing a scoped rifle from a moving vehicle is very challenging, and it should be done only as a last resort and if no other weapon is available. However, you should be able to fight with your rifle if the situation dictates it. If a rifle doesn't permit the use of open sights, the scope must be dialed to the lowest power setting possible, thus widening the field of view. All through the moving-vehicle drills most of the rifles performed well. Three ARs suffered the same problem of double feed, which is attributable to the AR-type magazine design. When a vehicle bobs and rocks over rough surfaces, it causes the bottom of a mag to strike the surface under it, causing a round to be released into the action and jamming the gun. It happens without exception during every class. To counter this, students using AR rifles must have a higher rest for their rifles and pay attention to the relation of a magazine to the surface under it.

When we were done with the counter-ambush drills, we moved on to the final series of exercises: long-range marksmanship. The class moved to the longest distance allowable, and several metal silhouette targets were set at 350 to 500 meters

with 50-meter intervals. Students then took turns engaging targets, working their way from closest to farthest. Great attention was paid to holdovers for both the elevation and windage as a slight crosswind suddenly picked up. Students then engaged targets rapidly in random order as I called them out. That's where the previous memorization of their holdovers came in handy because I did not allow any BDC manipulation. Everyone did very well and hit all his targets. The hardest target to hit was the 500-meter silhouette, because it was set in the shade against direct sunlight. Just another slice of reality. Nevertheless, after overcoming the struggle of identifying the target, everyone was able to put some lead on it.

And just like that the two-day class was over. Overall, the Soviet Spetsnaz Sniper Winter Weather Course was a great success. The weather cooperated, and the students shot extremely well in spite of being cold and out of their comfort zones. I am sure they walked away from this class not only better marksmen, but also better educated in their rifles and gear with solid knowledge of what it takes to survive and operate in an environment that is less than hospitable. I guess if there were one thing to take away from the Winter Weather Class, it would be that rifles and gear play equally important parts. Though everyone made it through the course, doubtless the next time the same students will be even better prepared and better equipped for it. One thing this outing did was open some eyes and raise some eyebrows. It sure made the participants look differently at their guns and kit.

GUNFIGHTING WITH THE
KALASHNIKOV

LEARN TO RUN THE AK THE WAY IT WAS INTENDED.

BY GABE SUAREZ

At Suarez International, we began building our Kalashnikov rifle program starting with a clean slate and backward planning—everything from where we wanted to be and what we wanted to be able to do. I wouldn't say that we reinvented the wheel, but we didn't want anything on that wheel that was unnecessary.

Specifically, we did not want to hold over AR-centric, police-centric or pistol-centric thinking. We discussed our needs with combat veterans and those attending SWAT events, as well as civilian and military events. This included contacts made from several armies, both U.S. and foreign—Russian Spetsnaz, Spanish Legion, British Ma-

rines, French Foreign Legion, Swiss, German, Serbian. The picture we ended up with did not look anything at all like a typical American urban rifle class.

We have been working with and teaching the Kalashnikov system at our facility for six years. Our material has been taught to hundreds of civilian shooters as well as to various

The rifle is a physical firearm. All skills should be robust and functional during physical exertion.

U.S. military personnel and contractors. They in turn have shared the material with their families, teammates and students. But I still run into misunderstandings about these rifles and how to operate them to their highest efficiency.

The first thing that a Kalashnikov operator must understand is that the Kalashnikov is not an AR-15, and it should not be run as one. Here are the essential skills you need to develop.

1. Learn to mount the rifle quickly, smoothly and uniformly so the gun always points where you want it to. Think of a sporting clays shooter who takes great pains to make sure his shotgun fits right. Your mount of the rifle should fit your upper body to the gun and present a consistent and uniform physical placement and visual index on the sights.

2. Learn to disengage the selector lever off Safe as you mount the rifle. Use the middle and index fingers of the firing hand to accompish this. Once you have disengaged the safety, do not be tempted to flick it on and off, back and forth. The only place I have seen that practice is here in the U.S. People do that because it is a holdover from the days when shooting instructors were trying to sell everyone on the 1911. It is a poor practice and likely to get you killed. Carry the rifle on

Operating the charging handle is done in one of three ways: under the receiver, over the receiver and with the shooting hand as needed.

The author demonstrates the infamous "AK pushup" with the South African .223 Kalashnikov.

Operators need to test their AK gun-handling skills off the square range. Here a student reloads during a bounding drill with his team.

Safe, but when the time comes to fight, disengage the safety and leave it off for the duration of the fight. Simple is better.

3. Learn to keep the trigger finger at the natural limit of extension.

4. Learn to reload the rifle under duress. I did not say speedload the rifle. Specifically, we should clarify the concepts of tactical, emergency and speed reloading.

Tactical reloading was first written about by H.W. McBride in his famous book, *A Rifle-*man Went to War. It was later publicized by Chuck Taylor, who prescribed it for a lull in the fight. To point of fact, while Taylor taught a speedload that jettisoned an empty magazine for a pistol, he was dead against it for the rifle, teaching instead to retain empty or partial magazines for later use.

When developing the material for our AK program, I queried the members at WarriorTalk for instances of an actual speedload saving anyone in a fight. While there were many stories of people reloading after the fight or reloading behind cover, no one was aware of any event in which the good guy was saved by being able to pull off the magazine-jettisoning typical speedload that so much training time seems to be spent on.

The only place you see shooters drop magazines on the range as a default practice is here in the U.S. Infantrymen around the world and operators who do not have extensive resources or supply lines make a habit of retaining their magazines. As one Special Forces

Operating the safety is fundamental to the system. Rather than seek technical shortcuts, learn the rifle as it is issued. Extend your fingers...

...then press down to release the safety.

For most efficient use, learning the rifle ambidextrously is a huge asset in the real world. To transfer it, move the butt-stock over to the other shoulder, then transfer your hand position.

soldier with experience operating with the northern alliance in Afghanistan told me, "You can get more ammo, but you may not get more magazines." So unless you have an armored Suburban filled with extra magazines or a Black Hawk helicopter dropping by with more, try to retain your spent and partial magazines.

Take out the onboard one, stow it, and replace it with a new one. The ability to change magazines is a staple that will allow you to keep the firearm loaded and reduce malfunctions in one maneuver.

5. Learn to run the bolt. Rather than spending money to redesign your AK to run like an FAL or an AR, learn to run the rifle as it is. The bolt goes back and then runs forward. Simple, isn't it? Train to go over the top of the receiver as well as underneath it. This maneuver should be a part of any reload or magazine-change process. It also serves as a hasty chamber check when you grab the rifle and go.

6. Learn trigger reset. Do this dry at first, then make it a habitual live-fire method. Press the trigger, hold it back while you run the bolt (in dry-fire mode), then slowly release it forward until you feel and hear the rifle reset. Then press the trigger again. Continue with this until it is reflexive. Repeat it live fire. Slapping a trigger may seem faster, but this will lead to missing your shots.

7. Learn to keep the rifle in operation. The major part of this need is addressed in No. 4, but we need to understand what to do should the rifle stop

The controls on the Kalashnikov are not dependent on fine motor skills and can be operated even when one is near frostbite.

The Kalashnikov system is very easy to learn and operate, far more so than many western designs.

The reloading process is simple and stressproof, handled with the rifle high in your workspace so you can view the battle area as you reload.

working. While Kalashnikovs will malfunction, this is rare compared with the incidence in other platforms. If the Kalashnikov stops firing, it may be due to a malfunction, but more likely it is due simply to running out of ammunition.

The common solution is to look at the chamber area and visually verify what is going on with the firearm. Once the problem has been determined, the operator must choose the appropriate solution from a number of possibilities. The

problem with this method is that it requires too much evaluation and decision time before a solution is put into practice. It is also unworkable for close-range problems due to the excessive time required to complete it. This method is also unworkable in reduced light when you cannot see what the problem is. The Kalashnikov system affords the operator some short cuts to get his rifle back in the fight that may not be available to someone using a different system.

Here is what I teach our students for malfunction solutions with an AK. It is sort of a flow chart or a decision ladder and is compliant with Hick's Law.

Stimulus: The rifle stops working, as evidenced by a dead trigger.

Thought Response: Are you inside pistol range (usually 25 yards for the average operator)?

If yes, transition to the pistol and eliminate the target. If no, get behind cover and fix the rifle.

What could be simpler? The distance-interval decision is

Ambidextrous work while moving is practiced to cover points along a 360-degree environment.

All 70 million Kalashnikovs around the world work the same, so learn the system and you'll know how to operate any of them. Here we see a Yugo 7.62x39 shooting next to a Bulgarian 5.45x39.

specifically fight-focused, not gun-focused. The goal is to eliminate the target, not necessarily to fix the gun.

Here is how we teach fixing the rifle. If the AK has stopped working, it is likely due to being out of ammo, so we fix that. But considering that there may be a failure to fire or eject, though this is less likely than an empty magazine, we simply reload the rifle with a fresh magazine. The process is this: old magazine out and stowed, new magazine in, run the bolt. That is our initial, immediate action. It is a robust solution, easy to remember, reliant on gross motor skills and sweeping in what it will clear.

If that fixes the rifle, you will know when you try to fire again and usually immediately after the clearance. If the rifle fires, you carry on with the mission of eliminating the target. If it does not fire, move to the secondary immediate action, which is to unload and reload the rifle. Remove the onboard magazine (and actually keep it in hand), work the bolt a few times, reinsert the magazine, and run the bolt one final time to chamber a round. Again, if this fixes the rifle, you will know when you try to fire. Ninety-nine percent of all stoppages with this platform will be solved quickly and efficiently in this manner.

There are two other possible stoppages that we should address in the spirit of thoroughness. The first is a fired case being thrown back into the receiver/trigger area. It doesn't happen often, but I have seen it a handful of times over the years, so it should be addressed. If you follow the process we described and the rifle is still hung up, remove the top cover and repeat the secondary immediate action of unloading and reloading, except this time without the top cover. This will dislodge anything stuck inside the receiver.

The final consideration is that anything man-made can break, and actual parts breakage, while rare in a Kalashnikov, can still happen and lock up the rifle. Thus if you have tried the three steps we discussed and the rifle is still inoperative, it's time to seek alternative solutions to target elimination because your rifle is no longer part of the solution.

The Kalashnikov is prolific in America now, and we are seeing many accessories for it. Some are very good, and others are not. I would suggest avoiding anything that changes the basic structure of the rifle's controls. The safety lever, bolt charging handle and magazine release should be left operationally as-is. This is due to one of the reasons we began working with the AK-47 in the first place. It is a prolific rifle not only in the U.S. but all over the world, and the rifle you grab to fight with may not be your specially prepared one. So rather than try to change those controls to fit current fashions, you should learn to run the basic rifle as-issued. When you have to pick up a dead terrorist's rifle, you will be glad you learned this.

The Kalashnikov rifle has taken America by storm and become one of the most widely accepted platforms in the arena of black rifles. Accept it for what it is, and learn to run it like it was intended. In the end you will not only have the most robust and reliable infantry rifle the world has ever seen, you will have the skill set to match. For more information on training, visit suarezinternational store.com.

There are other systems that emulate the Kalashnikov, such as the VZ-58. This fine rifle works almost the same as an AK, and the skill set transfers over well.

AUTOMATS IN AUSTIN

REVERSE ENGINEERING THE AK
GUNFIGHT WITH SONNY PUZIKAS.

BY STEVE MILES

The desolate bay we were training in could have been anywhere. High-bermed dirt walls reached up to an overcast sky, blocking any view of the surrounding terrain. The only thing that gave away that this was a private range outside Austin in the Texas Hill Country was a lone Longhorn cow standing near the entrance gate.

I was here to train with Sonny Puzikas, a man rather unique among U.S.-based AK instructors. Sonny is the real deal: a Soviet Spetsnaz commando, a living relic of the Cold War. While President Reagan stood at the Berlin Wall and famously demanded, "Mr. Gorbachev, tear down this wall!" Sonny was preparing to defend that bastion of the Soviet empire. It's an epic understatement to say times have changed.

I was looking for answers about the AK, the rifle I had come to regard highly while serving in Iraq. To a career U.S. soldier raised on the M16, the AK is an enigma. Its controls seem misplaced. Its edges are rough. Magazine changes feel awkward. And forget about cheekweld. But despite all that, there was one redeeming quality to the AK that made it golden: It was the rifle that worked.

I had witnessed the incredible reliability of the AK in combat, and it seemed to me that behind the wisdom of that reliability, there must also be some intelligence behind the other design features. Sonny had those answers—and much more. This is a story not only about the AK hardware, but also the human software that runs the AK to its fullest potential.

"I need a volunteer," Sonny said. He spoke in clear English with just the slightest trace of a Russian accent. Several attendees raised their hands. With a hint of a smile, Sonny gestured at a large student from a local SWAT unit and said, "You will do."

Nineteen men (including me) and one woman were almost halfway through the first day of a weekend AK gunfighting seminar and had yet to fire a single round. We started the morning with AK calisthenics, warm-up exercises ingeniously designed to showcase the strength of the weapon and give Sonny an assessment of our strength. Then Sonny got us moving with horizontal displacement drills, how to get out of the line of fire in a hurry.

He added complexity by asking us to do additional tasks as we moved, such as magazine changes, shoulder transitions and malfunction drills. Now it was time to work vertical displacement, but after three hours some of the students were starting to drag. Many had started the day wearing a lot of extra gear, and quickly getting up and down while performing additional tasks seemed to be challenging. Sonny sensed the frustration.

"I submit to you that every one of you can do this if given the proper motivation," Sonny said. He positioned his volunteer out in front of the group. "When you sense the threat, I want you to perform the vertical displacement while simultaneously drawing your pistol and simulate firing at that target." He gestured toward a cardboard image of a terrorist.

"You will know, comrade," Sonny said. And then he demonstrated something he couldn't have learned in the Soviet Union. Grasping his AK by the barrel and raising it above his head in the manner of a baseball slugger, he drew it back and then swung for the fences.

The student dropped out of the line of the swing and presented his pistol just as he had been instructed. Flawlessly. The class applauded, and the student got up, looking somewhat surprised at himself.

"This is Reverse Engineering. Prioritizing movement first. This is what I am teaching you today."

The contrasts could not be starker. Not many men awarded Soviet medals for bravery and valor in combat are also credited with helping sell a billion dollars' worth of video games. Millions of video gamers have seen Sonny's movements, and they have tried to kill him as well. Sonny's gunfighting movements were captured on video, digitized and programmed into the movements of Spetsnaz characters in the hit "Call of Duty" video game series. Sonny has also been featured on cable TV military-themed shows, such as "Weaponology" and "Deadliest Warrior," and he recently completed filming his second Hollywood movie.

But all this entertainment success hasn't gone to his head. It's 9:00 p.m., and he's working as a firefighter in suburban Dallas when I call him for a telephone interview after the seminar. He's just back from an emergency call-out. I can hear other firemen cheering at a football game on the TV in the background. "Tell me about Reverse Engineering," I said.

"It's a mistake to think that you are going to always act first in a gunfight, that you will always be able to see threats before they act, that you will be able to draw your weapon and engage your enemy before he even has his weapon out. It's a dream, and it will remain so, particularly for civilians," Sonny said.

"The premise of a gunfight is that you are being shot at. It's not that you are shooting at them. You are going to have to react to a gunfight in progress, meaning that someone is already engaging you. If your baseline skill is to stand there, draw the weapon, establish the stance, point the weapon, take a deep breath and squeeze the trigger after acquiring a correct sight picture, I submit that you are never going to see the end of the fight because it's going to get dark and quiet for you. From that realization, I decided I was going to spend significant time teaching people to move and displace first and then fuse the weapon skills in with simultaneous movement. That's how Reverse Engineering came about."

Sonny's class had certainly been full of movement. I could recall almost none of the "stand

In his "Reverse Engineering" method, Sonny provides some motivation for a student to prioritize movement over marksmanship.

and deliver" method I had seen in other classes. "It seems like you are prioritizing movement over marksmanship. Is that correct?" I asked.

"You can live by movement, and you can die by movement," Sonny said. "If I have a good hard cover, do I have to move? No. This is the problem: If you don't have the skill to move but need to move, you are in deep trouble. If I have the skill to move, but I need to be stationary, there's much less skill involved being stationary and shooting. If we spend time learning to index the weapon with our body, or intuitively use part of the front sight, we can be effectively accurate within the distances common to engagements, absolutely. When you have the ability to be dynamic and place effective fire on the move, I submit that you are light years ahead of most opponents."

At the seminar most of the students had previous tactical training experience, and many already seemed quite proficient handling the AK. But it quickly became apparent that developing that ability to shoot effectively on the move was going to require an entirely different skill-set than most students had brought with them.

"Let's be honest," he said, "the AK, regardless of which caliber you are shooting, is not a cannon. It's not that hard to handle the recoil, and in my opinion, most people are definitely overdoing fighting the recoil. They have a tense body, what some call putting a strong structure behind the weapon. I want you to work with the weapon versus trying to fight what the weapon does."

By this point we had already rapid-fired a few rounds into the targets so Sonny could get an assessment of our shooting skills. He directed us to line up again in front of the same targets. This time he told us to make a V-shape with our support hand, rest the handguard of the firearm in that V, grasp the pistol grip with the other hand, but not touch the rifle with our shoulder, face or any other part of our bodies. Instead, we should just line up the sights, apply a slight forward pressure at the pistol grip and squeeze the trigger.

"If we allow it to, the bullet will go where the weapon is pointed. It is the tension in our bodies applied to the weapon that causes that bullet to miss the target."

Expecting that the minimally supported rifle would fly back, many students flinched as they pulled the trigger. But it didn't fly back. In fact, students were astounded by how fast the rifle was back on target after each shot. Even more surprising, the groups fired by the students were visibly tighter than their initial assessment group.

"The AK was designed to be an all-purpose battle rifle, not a specialist precision rifle," Sonny said. "The comb of the stock was not designed for you to get a Western-style cheekweld on it. I submit to you that at common engagement ranges you do not need that kind of cheekweld where the shoulders are raised, creating a very tense upper platform, with head pulled in and down to establish sight alignment. In fact, often you do not want it in the CQB realm.

"In Soviet rifle instruction the head is leaned forward instead of pulling it in, maintaining your shoulders loose and relaxed," Sonny continued. "Extending your head forward allows better mobility in your upper platform, which allows you quicker work in the 360-degree environment, such as ambidextrous transfers from shoulder to shoulder. Drawing the shoulders up and keeping a very tight structure also degrades your peripheral vision, creating some blind spots that might affect your ability to see obstacles during movement."

And then came the movement: Left, right, up, down, while firing from the right shoulder, firing from the left shoulder, magazine changes and pistol transitions with the right and left hands while moving. It was dizzying at first, but after some time my movements began to look more dynamic than dyslexic.

"You must move as the fight requires, not as your lack of skill dictates," said Sonny.

SONNY PUZIKAS

Sonny Puzikas grew up in the Soviet Socialist Republic of Lithuania. He became familiar with the AK at an early age, in paramilitary volunteer groups. ("You signed up if you wanted to skip biology and instead go to the shooting range.") He joined the Soviet Ministry of Internal Affairs (MVD) and was selected for duty in a regional special purpose unit (Spetsnaz). As the Soviet Union entered its twilight in the late 1980s and early '90s, Sonny's unit acted multiple times against internal threats to the regime. He was later selected to join an elite national-level Spetsnaz unit, and in the final bloody days of the Soviet Union, he went into combat against separatists and Islamic militants at locations across the country.

Following the collapse of the Soviet Union, Sonny immigrated to the U.S. "We can say it was time to change life and look for better options," he said. In the U.S. he worked in the personal security industry before becoming a trainer, actor, firefighter and video game icon.

Today, Sonny presents his unique perspective on the AK rifle and gunfighting in private and public seminars worldwide.

During the class, Sonny used an AKS-74 custom built by Rifle Dynamics (702-860-7774, rifledynamics.com) of Las Vegas, Nev.

By the end of the first day the hands of many of the students were showing the effects of repeated manipulations of the AK's controls. An AK usually comes from the factory with more than a few sharp edges and points. Holding up nicked and scratched hands, one student asked, "Is this normal?"

"Yes," Sonny answered. "When you work the AK over and over again in training, you are going to affect your skin to a certain degree. I really don't see it as a problem. The AK was designed to function in all environmental conditions. This includes wet, iced up and even covered with blood, as you can see. Many Western weapons are overly ergonomic, and when small, rounded controls are handled in less than optimum environmental conditions, I submit you will have what are called 'operator errors,' but this is the supposed ergonomic design contributing to those errors.

"And besides, all those sharp edges, the charging handle, the front sight post, the curved magazine, they definitely give you some nice advantages during hand-to-hand combat or crowd control."

Sonny arrived at the range on both days with a white paper cup of coffee. He held the cup without spilling any of the coffee, even while demonstrating some very dynamic and explosive movements. There was a smoothness to his movement, an articulation whereby his upper body seemed to float independently over his legs. The second day of the seminar Sonny introduced us to a very unconventional drill intended to develop this same sort of smoothness in our shooting.

"I need another volunteer." Sonny said this in a calm voice that downplayed the drama of the moment. By this point everyone knew volunteering to help Sonny demonstrate a drill was going to be a memorable experience. And either because of this or in spite of it, several students raised their hands. Sonny selected one of them and asked him to lie on his back.

"This is a very efficient way to learn to shoot from a moving platform, whether that platform is a train or boat you are standing on, or if the platform is you moving. It instantly teaches perfect shooting posture, isolating the upper firing platform from the lower body."

After some additional explanation, Sonny stepped up and onto the stomach of his volunteer, charged his AK and emptied the magazine in a rapid string of shots. Despite his lower body shifting to maintain balance on his less than stable volunteer, the barrel of Sonny's AK scarcely came off the target at all. Seamlessly transitioning to his pistol, Sonny unleashed another rapid-fire volley for good measure.

After much dry-fire training and implementing some additional safety constraints, the students tried the live-fire drill while standing on one another. It was remarkable: After just a few shots, all the students were standing in nearly identical correct posture. The task of managing

Students work drills combining vertical displacement, shoulder transfers and magazine changes.

Two students run a live-fire team drill showcasing bilateral weapons handling, firing from each shoulder.

recoil while maintaining balance on the shifting platform was an incredibly effective teaching tool. Some of the students were skeptical before they tried it, but they had nothing but positive remarks about the drill afterward.

By the end of the second day students were moving through Sonny's drills with some fluidity, and we had begun exploring the applications of bilateral rifle handling in the team environment. One of the students voiced concern that Sonny's methodology did not include maintaining the AK's selector on Safe at all times except when actively firing.

"There's the safety switch, and then there's being safe. And one does not require the other. I know in the West there is endless play with the safety: You have the target in the sights you disengage the safety, you fire and you reengage the safety. In the Soviet military, the safety play was absent. As soon as the rifle came off the sling, the safety switch was disengaged, and until it was absolutely certain the engagement was over that safety would not come back on. People may say that is dangerous, but to me, playing too much with the safety puts too much reliance on mechanical devices to keep us from making a mistake. Real safety comes from training."

At the end of the second day, we circled up and shared our comments about the seminar. It had been tough training: on our bodies, our egos and,

Students perform a drill to isolate lower-body movement from the firing platform.

most of all, our expectations about what gunfight training should look like. For me, the weekend had surpassed my expectations of learning more about running the AK and provided me with a new perspective on gunfighting I hadn't expected.

Before we ended the event, Sonny explained what he really wanted everyone to take away from his training: "One thing I would wish for you all is the ability to examine. Examine not just what is being taught in the seminar, but to examine the reality you face. There are so many gunfighting dogmas that are only remotely applicable to our own circumstances. Are there things a military commando can pass along to a civilian? Sure. But everyone's situation is unique: their skills or lack thereof, their physical conditioning or lack thereof, their equipment, the layout of their house and a million other variables. I really want guys to be able to think for themselves about what is the reality they face and train accordingly."

Sonny gives the final briefing to two students before running a live-fire team drill.

Students demonstrate one of Sonny's vertical displacement methods, the "Modified Prone Position."